# Voices, Vision and Vitality

## Redesigning Small Schools

# Earle Newton

and

# Patti Newton

Detselig Enterprises Ltd.
Calgary, Alberta

**Canadian Cataloguing in Publication Data**

Newton, Earle, 1933-
Voices, visions and vitality

ISBN 1-55059-047-2

1. Education, Rural – Canada, Western.
2. Rural schools – Canada, Western Administration.
I. Newton, Patti.    II. Title.
LC5148.C2N49  1992    370.19'346'09712    C92-091852-2

Detselig Enterprises Ltd.
#210 1220 Kensington Rd. N.W.
Calgary, Alberta
T2N 3P5

Detselig appreciates financial assistance for its 1992 publishing program from Canada Council and Alberta Foundation for the Arts.

Printed in Canada        SAN 115-0324        ISBN 1-55059-047-2

*This book is dedicated to the work, life and memories of our parents and grandparents, who were community builders, homemakers, farmers, ranchers, grain elevator agents, teachers and merchants in rural Alberta and Saskatchewan.*

# Contents

## Section One
## —Threats and Opportunities

## Section Two
## —Voices

## Section Three
## —Vision and Vitality

## Section Four
## —Putting it All Together

# List of Tables and Figures

# Preface

This book is a valuable resource supporting the study of education in rural communities in Canada, particularly Western Canada. Unlike most other books on rural schools or schools in small towns which focus on macro issues such as the changing rural landscape and migration patterns, this book focuses on the micro issues of student, parent and school staff responses. The book then takes these micro issues and characterizes a learning organization, outlines how to capitalize on advantages, and suggests how to turn negative aspects of community into positives ones.

Over the past decade and a half, I have searched for Canadian resources to support an upper level undergraduate course entitled, "Issues in Rural Education," and found very few; none in text format. I searched for a book that would be compatible with my goals: to provide future teachers—one-third of whom will likely end up teaching in a small or rural community—with conceptual tools to understand community dynamics (including all sides of the debate on the purposes of schools in small communities), with a greater understanding of themselves, their values and attitudes, and with an experience enabling them to bring the above together in a reflective term paper.

At one point I developed my own materials that I used extensively, but since moving from British Columbia to Alberta, found the material lacking Alberta, or prairie province specifics. This book is terrific in that it draws extensively from anecdotal records and data from systematic research of Alberta and Saskatchewan. It provides the reader with a greater under-standing of people most intimately concerned with rural schools, students, parents and teachers.

I found integrating each chapter of the book into the course delightful. Students were asked to work in groups and present the information of each chapter to the class using strategies involving the class in active participation. Over the next year I will prepare a set of class activities that focus on the numerous tables of detailed data presented in each chapter. These data help bridge theory and practice in my course. The book has provided my course with a link between rural sociological concepts (which I studied in the United States), educational concepts (which I studied in British Columbia), and rural Alberta (which I am to focus on at the University of Calgary).

I wish to acknowledge the authors of this text for seeing this need and for all the work that this book entailed.

Thomas D. Gougeon

# 1

# Introduction

*I feel parents have no say in happenings at school.*

- a parent

A major purpose of this book is to emphasize the importance of listening to people who live in sparsely populated areas. We shall begin by sharing some comments from parents, students and teachers.

❖　❖　❖

## Parents

*Bearpaw elementary has one of the best staffed schools in the system . . . my kids like school, like their teachers, like the atmosphere in Bearpaw . . . they smile a lot, laugh a lot and read three years above their grade level. Deerfoot lacks character, discipline, well-trained staff, facilities, equipment, atmosphere . . . It's a killer of creative education. I'll move before sending my kids to Deerfoot.*

- Parent comment regarding possible<br>closure of a K-6 school with 83 students.

*I wish there wasn't so much animosity among community people. . . .*

*If it's best for children, it's up to the adults to get their act together.*

- Native leader commenting about the<br>possibility of an integrated school on an Indian reserve.

*They tell you one thing to your face and never follow through. If confronted with a serious situation at a school, they totally evade the question at hand.*

## Students

*Some of my teachers are really interested in my work, but some teachers don't seem to care.*

*There seems to be a lack of two-way communication and mutual respect between young people and adults both in the community and at school.*

- Future Farmer of America (1990)
identifying issues in rural education.

*We are often treated as children and not respected for what we do. We are often remembered by our mistakes, but never rewarded for our efforts to make things better.*

*For the most part I like the school the way it is (K-12, 54 students, 5 teachers). I enjoy all of my teachers and the way they run the school. I would like to change the number of subjects you can take to give students a better opportunity in the 'real' world.*

## Teachers

*You can ask any one of them for help. It's a staff that gets along really well inside of school and outside – you have to in a small place.*

*It's part of the job. Why can't you come out and coach hockey? The community does put a lot of pressure on – they expect a lot more than we can give.*

*We tend to be working under fairly satisfactory conditions compared to some other schools and towns of the same size. Morale in a school depends on staff and the longer a staff stays in one place, usually the poorer they get along as a group.*

*They appear only when there is a problem. When the superintendent visits the school, the teachers wonder 'What's wrong now?"*

❖     ❖     ❖

These voices, the authors' experience in rural school communities and the literature agree on a major point—there are both advantages and disadvantages to small schools in sparsely populated areas. Warren Hathaway provided a helpful review of literature in a paper given at a recent Prairie Forum on Rural Education in Brandon, Manitoba. How could you, the reader, add to his summary shown in Table 1.1? Are there points of disagreement? Are there some aspects for continuing dialogue?

The authors believe that in periods of economic hardship, urban migration and general disillusionment with leadership, people in rural school-communities tend to get bogged down in difficulties to the point that they are often unable to realize the many potential advantages of small schools.  We need to remember that much current practice such as individualized instruction, independent learning, flexible scheduling, peer tutoring and teaching, non-gradedness, co-operative education, and school-community partnerships originated in small schools. Current emphasis on life-long learning, education program continuity, community-based curriculum, shared governance, partnerships, parental involvement, environmental studies and technology are particularly promising for education in small school-communities.

The authors lived the first eighteen years of our lives in rural areas of Alberta and Saskatchewan, Canada. Since then they have been enriched by a combined period of over sixty years of working with leaders of small schools at the system, provincial, national and international level. Recent experience at rural education centres in Colorado and Western Australia have added greatly to our perspective and understanding. We have reflected on our lifetime of involvement in bringing to light important beliefs which provide the themes for this book:

1. Many rural schools are into on-going development but some are not. While many are "moving," others are "stuck."

2. It is time to shift emphasis from single innovations to multiple changes within broader planning processes, and from the school as the unit of change to school systems.

3. The title of this book reflects the view that listening to the voices of all partners and developing a shared vision through stronger leadership are central to school and system development. Improved listening, sharing and leading are relatively inexpensive.

4. Recent literature and developments related to strategic planning, change processes, leadership, performance indicators, monitoring, evaluation and learning organizations are particularly promising for small school-communities.

5. Typical school communities in sparsely populated areas have the human resources to launch or accelerate school development but higher expectations, appropriate support and networking are vital.

6. There is no quick fix. We do not advocate a cookbook, step-by-step approach to leadership. Instead, we believe cyclical processes of thinking, relating to others and planning in an action-oriented environment result in "learning by doing."

 7. Schools move when leaders can link global and local events, can integrate "top down" with "bottom up" initiatives and can "think big but start small." We advocate a holistic, integrated approach to school development. We emphasize insiders' views and draw attention to the importance of contextual factors.

8. There are new challenges and new opportunities for educational leadership for schooling in sparsely populated areas. There **are** alternatives and choices.

## Table 1.1 Advantages and Disadvantages of Small Rural Schools

| Factor | Advantages | Disadvantages |
|---|---|---|
| Financial Administration | • Less bureaucracy & red tape<br>• Flatter organization<br>• Principal knows students | • Higher than average costs<br>• Principal has few peers with whom to interact<br>• Lack of administrative assistance makes it necessary for principal to engage in administrative details |
| Teachers | • Lower pupil/teacher ratio<br>• Teacher knows students<br>• Teacher closer to overall administration of school and more aware of administrative concerns<br>• Better able to integrate curriculum concepts across multiple subjects | • Must prepare and provide more courses<br>• Teachers have few peers with whom to interact |
| Students | • More involvement in extra-curricular activities<br>• More leadership opportunities<br>• Achievement is equivalent to achievement in larger urban schools | • Students experience modest culture shock when moving out of the community for further education or employment |
| Community | • School is centre of community<br>• High levels of community support for school | • Small school may resist change<br>• Lack of cultural diversity limits opportunities for broad socialization |
| Guidance | • Teachers able to offer personal guidance and counselling | • School may be unduly influenced by community values |
| Atmosphere | • More humane and productive<br>• More involvement of students, teachers and community in co-operative ventures means better attitudes and higher expectations | • Smallness and remoteness may lead to feelings of inferiority |

| Program | • Results on achievement tests are often as good as results in larger schools and in some cases better (science may be an exception)<br>• Good achievement potential in the affective domain | • Limited program choice<br>• Limited resources<br>• Little up-to-date technology<br>• Lack of specialists capable of demonstrating excellence in areas of curriculum (e.g., fine arts, athletics, academics) |
| Other | • Greater community awareness and acceptance of school policy | |

Source: Warren Hathaway, "Rural Education: Challenges and Opportunities," Prairie Forum on Rural Education, Brandon, Manitoba, November, 1990.

## Challenges

A large majority of rural students, particularly in lower grades, are happy with their teachers. Most parents rate teachers, principals, bus drivers and support staff highly. In other words, most people view learning and teaching and general school operations quite positively. Most problems arise at the planning part of the school enterprise. Students think no one listens to them outside of the classroom; staff relations are often strained; school-community communication is frequently inadequate; superintendents are seen to appear only when there is a problem; very few stakeholders are aware of what the school board does or how they do it. These conditions are addressed directly by Carkhuff in his book, *The Age of the New Capitalism* (1988). In addition, to emphasize on human capital (good people who are getting better) and on information capital (organizations with relevant, current information move ahead), he draws attention to three levels of operation within organizations:

- Thinking individually

- Relating in groups

- Planning at the organizational level

Our work in rural schools has convinced us that the parties concerned are strong at the level of thinking individually. Difficulties arise in linking those individual efforts to action in groups and to planning at the school system level.

## This Book

This book is focused on listening to the voices of partners, formulating a shared vision for schooling and providing leadership that will revitalize schools in sparsely populated areas. Themes are based on Carkhuff's idea of establishing and strengthening the connections among individual thinking, relating in groups and planning at the school system level. A strategic planning model is used to integrate these components.

In Section One of the book we present strategic planning as the most promising approach we know of to seize the opportunities and to reduce the threats of current small school-community contexts. We use the word "strategic" advisedly to highlight the fact that things don't just happen, that learning by experience alone is not enough and that the dynamics and complexity of schooling today require deliberate, concerted efforts to allay feelings of helplessness. Strategy is required even to cope let alone lead.

Voices are stressed in Section Two. One school system context is described in order to provide interpretive validity. Survey results from the Big Valley system are reported in considerable detail in order to give readers background for reflection.

The emphases on context and voices come together in Section Three with chapters on leadership, change processes, monitoring and evaluation. All of these topics are crucial in strategic planning. Monitoring and evaluation are also directly related to current social priorities for information and accountability.

The final chapter includes a one page summary of thinking, relating and planning for each of the six phases in the strategic planning model we present. We indicate how leaders for schooling have to be "simultaneously loose-tight" and how the concept of a "learning organization" holds promise for small school-communities.

In this book the authors have shared many promising developments in small school-communities (under 5 000 people) from Canada, the United States and Australia. They have related relevant literature to the rural context within a strategic planning process. Emphasis is on *leadership, voices and vision*.

The authors have taken care to make this book readable, concise and sufficiently data based. It is primarily intended for school superintendents, other educational administrators and elected officials who are typically "on the run," always short of time for reading and impatient with written material which is not to the point and practical. The book demonstrates that in every school system there are gaps between "what is" and "what could be." These gaps provide a natural beginning to refocus practice and to take initiative.

People looking for "pat answers" and "quick fixes" should read no further. Administrators anxious to get "promoted to the city" are not likely willing to assume the risks inherent in visionary leadership, and should give this book away— it does not offer advice for "putting out fires." If you are a public or professional person with a hunch that things could be better in your schools, read on. If you see living, learning and leading as an integrated adventure we think this book will support and encourage you.

*Too often there has been far too much emphasis on empire-building, playing power politics, and not enough foresight with emphasis on what is good for all students.*

- a parent

## References

Carkhuff, R. (1988). *The age of the new capitalism.* Amherst, MA: Human Resource Development Press, Inc.

Hathaway, W. (1990). *Rural education: Challenges and opportunities.* Paper presented to the Prairie Forum on Rural Education, Brandon, Manitoba, November.

# Threats and Opportunity

Threats to quality of life and effective schooling in sparsely populated areas are well known. Much less well known are the opportunities presented in such contexts for uniquely rewarding learning experiences for the total community. Our belief is that such benefits can be realized by strong leadership and effective strategic planning processes which include analyses of local contexts.

# 2

# Strategic Planning

*As a taxpayer I'm really frustrated paying for things I have no control over.*
                                                            - a parent

Planning is not new to us. We plan a weekend. We plan a holiday. We plan careers. The way we decorate our home, the car we buy, the goods we manufacture, the waters we fish and the trees we cut are likely all, more or less, in accordance with some plan which we have in mind or within which we must work. Basically planning means to consider our circumstances and to decide how we can best achieve what we desire. Selecting a program at a technical institute, opening a new store or assuming a mortgage are, in the final analysis, plans. Plans, then, are part of our life and they may be simple or complex, informal or formal. To a great extent they are a natural response to the challenges and opportunities we encounter.

The need for leaders in today's complex, rapidly changing world is to surface and to talk about the beliefs and assumptions which underlie our plans. For example, many readers will recall the early 1960s when 25 year mortgages at a low, fixed rate of interest were common—they were long term plans for paying for a house. Both the lender and the borrower were "locked in." In contrast, mortgages today are typically for from 6 months to 5 years with varying rates of interest and the option of paying lump sums—these are strategic plans with provision for both lenders and borrowers to make decisions as circumstances change. The 25 year mortgages were based upon assumptions of a stable, predictable society and the belief that people would maintain their aspirations, income, values and place of residence over long periods of time. Open, shorter term mortgages are designed to accommodate expected changes both in social conditions and in people.

Schools and curricula have, for at least a century, been based upon assumptions of a stable, predictable environment. Everyone was expected to go to school between ages 6 to 18, learn to spell "rhubarb" in grade 4, pass or fail at the end of the school year, and get a "good shot" of Tennyson, Shakespeare and Milton. Truth was absolute and enduring, schools were set and planning was long-term—at least such planning would have been considered appropriate—and simple, rational and step-by-step. Schools were closed to external factors and educational leaders alone solved problems if any surfaced. Parents and the public were assured by the profession if an issue arose, "Don't worry, we'll look after it."

Today, as we think of how to prepare young people for the next century, old assumptions underlying, and designed for, schooling are being called into question. Our experience, common sense and thoughts all help us to realize that there are very few absolutes in the world today. Stephen Hawking (1988) in *A Brief History of Time* points out that, even in the scientific world, virtually all knowledge is relative to time and space. David Suzuki in a recent television documentary, *The Nature of Things*, beautifully illustrated how there are patterns in turbulence (running water) and how there is unpredictability in patterns (the weather). Catch phrases such as "going with the flow," "rolling with the punches" and "thriving on chaos" (Tom Peters, 1988) reflect an increasing awareness of an exciting but unpredictable environment manifesting both patterns and uncertainty.

How are schools responding to the shift from absolute truth to relative truth, from stability to instability, from predictability to unpredictability, from hierarchy to flatter organizational structures and from fragmentation to integration? Eminent writers in curriculum are writing about curriculum for instability. A renowned authority in administration, Sergiovanni (1987), advocates a reflective practice approach to the principalship. In a book called *Productive School Systems for a Nonrational World*, Patterson, Purkey and Parker (1986) present persuasive arguments for strategic planning.

> *I think it's time that tantrums quit controlling the
> finances and common sense takes over.*
>
> - a parent

*interdependent / flow of info*

# What is Strategic Planning

Simply put, strategic planning is an information system that enables one to take changing conditions into consideration when making decisions and to link present action to visions of tomorrow. Compared to long-range planning, strategic planning is more likely to include visions of success, to focus on issues, to emphasize internal and external analysis, to be action oriented and to require on-going monitoring and evaluation. In Table 2.1 we have outlined the essential components and processes of strategic planning as we see it.

### Table 2.1 Strategic Planning

| Components | Processes |
|---|---|
| 1. Clarifying organizational mandates | • check mission statements, values, roles, responsibilities, human and financial resources<br>• create awareness of SP, clarify expectations<br>• select a team, decide on process<br>• who is the strongest advocate committed to "making it work?" |
| 2. External Analysis (Environmental Scanning) | • determine and consider trends and issues from the global to the local (Chapter 3 could be a starting point)<br>• identify opportunities and threats |
| 3. Internal Analysis | • hear the voices of students, parents, community, teachers, administrators, school boards<br>• identify strengths and weaknesses in "what is going on" from various perspectives |
| 4. Integration of Analyses | • leadership—"ideas of how things could be better"<br>• sketch alternative futures<br>• identify strategic issues in moving toward the vision |
| 5. Implementing | • plan for change<br>• determine quality indicators<br>• implement |
| 6. Monitoring- Evaluating | • monitor progress in relation to intentions and vision<br>• evaluate<br>• feed results into step 3 of the next SP cycle |

Writers emphasize different aspects of strategic planning. For example, McCune (1986) stresses that strategic planning enables the organization to better match changes in the external, global and community environments. She refers to a range of factors from fibre optics and biogenetics to ethnic diversity and more women in the work force. Bryson (1989) emphasizes the importance of a "champion" to be primarily responsible for the strategic planning process and an advisory board to guide it. He also believes that *strategic thinking* and *strategic acting* are even more important than strategic planning.

As with everything else these days, knowledge is temporary so strategic planning should not be viewed as being in a final form. The process undoubtedly has to be adapted to any particular context. It is dynamic  with many "ups and downs" and the need for adjustments along the way. Some developments from the state / provincial to the school level in aspects of strategic planning are reported so that we can think about our experiences in relation to what is going on elsewhere.

## Turning to Illustrations

The State of North Dakota has an Education Action Commission which includes public hearings to build consensus regarding the direction of public education. According to a paper in the fall of 1990 from the N.D. Consensus Council Inc., strategies for change included a state-wide vision and plan, revision of statutes that inhibit local creativity and accomplishment of what is envisioned, financial incentive for design improvements and school district reorganization, a search for additional funding and an expanded leadership role involving a broad range of stakeholders. A new definition of quality and learning emphasized a performance-based school accreditation system, a new definition of learning to include problem solving and career skills, performance assessment systems broader than standardized tests, an interdisciplinary curriculum which is community based, partnerships and additional support for professional staff.

The State of Western Australia in 1989 issued a policy bulletin for mandated school development plans and the following year for school decision making groups. The policy stipulates that school development plans must include:

- the purpose of the school

- indicators of the school's performance

- details of how monitoring will be done

- local and Ministry priorities

- how the priorities will be addressed

- allocation of resources to ensure effective outcomes

Central to this initiative is participation of parents. When a school decision-making group—made up of equal numbers of parents and staff representatives, with the principal as chair—is satisfied with a plan, it is to endorse the plan and then the principal also signs it and submits it to the District Superintendent. A document from the Ministry states, "Demonstrating accountability for educating a community's children is a difficult and complex task. All schools are required to demonstrate effectiveness through their school development plans."

## Figure 2.1 Model for Planning Cycle

In the province of Alberta the Ministry requires school systems to adopt and implement policies for the evaluation of students, teachers, programs, schools and systems. A related system review of Foothills School Division included a recommended model for a planning cycle which is shown below:

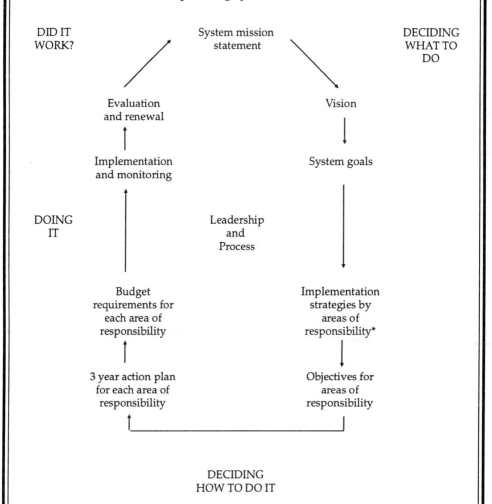

DID IT WORK?

System mission statement

DECIDING WHAT TO DO

Evaluation and renewal

Vision

Implementation and monitoring

System goals

DOING IT

Leadership and Process

Budget requirements for each area of responsibility

Implementation strategies by areas of responsibility*

3 year action plan for each area of responsibility

Objectives for areas of responsibility

DECIDING HOW TO DO IT

Developed by: C. Allan and E. Yates, 1989.

*Areas of responsibility are considered to be administration, curriculum, maintenance, finance, etc.

The Abbotsford Model for strategic planning in a school has been developed by School District 34 in Clearbrook, British Columbia. The model is shown on the following page (Figure 2-2). The Director of schools in a recent article states, "One must understand, however, that strategic planning requires flexibility; application of a rigid step-by-step process may be more destructive than productive. Each school must adopt the plan with a clear understanding of its specific attributes, and with a view to developing future directions for its situation." (p. 12, D. Truscott, *The Canadian School Executive*, October, 1989).

## Figure 2.2 Abbotsford Model for Strategic Planning

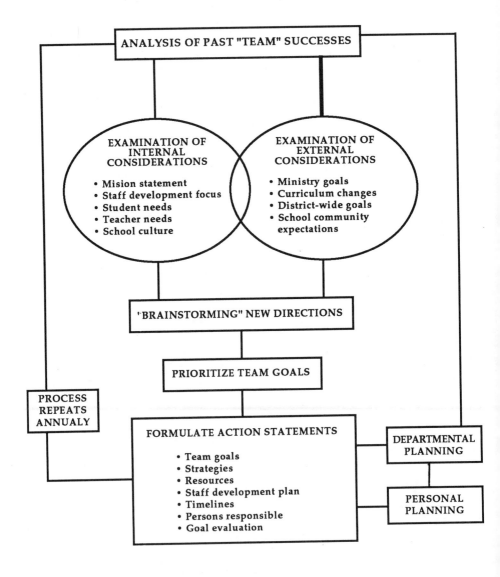

- School District 34, Clearbrook, B.C.

In the examples presented we see major efforts in three countries to utilize various aspects of strategic planning for the development of schools. We can see attempts to link the present with the future, internal analysis with environmental changes, the simple with the complex and information-based decision making with an overall planning process. The "strategic" aspect is prominent because some issues are more important (strategic) than others, not everything can be done at once, and there must be a plan (strategy) if implementation is to be successful.

What are your thoughts about strategic planning? What is the "fit" between approaches to strategic planning presented in this chapter and what you are already doing? Could more attention to strategic planning bring your school and community closer together and enable you to offer stronger leadership?

## Why Bother?

We believe that outcomes of strategic planning will include better schools and improved student learning. We are convinced that the emphasis on voices and vision will help to realize many potential advantages of  small schools. Actions will be directed toward the future and work will become increasingly meaningful as day-to-day efforts are linked to vision. All of this can happen more easily and more readily in small centres than in more complex, urban settings that tend to be depersonalized. Are you ready to do more, to lead, to forge ahead?

What of resources and risks? We believe that the human resources are in place. Parents and community want the best schooling possible and will work hard to contribute. Students want to be more involved in schooling. Teachers and administrators typically will, and do, "go the extra mile." We tend to be bogged down because we need to redesign schooling to build in more participative, futuristic, locally-relevant processes. We need to assign more of our present human resources to leadership and we need more respect and support for leadership. If people are involved, can see where the schools are headed, and can determine how far they have come in the last year, political risks will be minimized. Leaders will win support. We ought to aim higher for what can be accomplished in schools in sparsely populated areas. Let us not resign ourselves to decline or to what we did last year. In relation to small schools some things are worth fighting for.

*The Preferred Futures process is excellent . . . it does give a glimmer of hope.*

*– a teacher*

## References

Alberta Education (1991). *Vision for the nineties: A plan of action.* Edmonton: Government of Alberta.

Alberta Education (1989). *A System Review.* Calgary Regional Office, 1200 Rocky Mt. Plaza, 615 Macleod Trail, S.E., Calgary, Alberta, T2G 4T8.

Bryson, J.M. (1989). *Strategic planning for public and nonprofit organizations.* London: Jossey-Bass Publishers.

Hawking, S.W. (1988). *A brief history of time.* Toronto: Bantam Books.

McCune, S.D. (1986). *Guide to strategic planning for educators.* Alexandria, VA: Association for Supervision and Curriculum Development.

North Dakota Consensus Council Incorporated (1990). *Consensus building conflict resolution forum: Report to the Education Action Commission.* Bismarck, ND.

Parry, A. (1990). *Corporate and strategic planning.* Workshop materials presented to Alberta Education, Westridge, Alberta, October.

Patterson, N.L., Purkey, S.C. & Parker, J.V. (1986). *Productive school systems for a nonrational world.* Alexandria, VA: Association for Supervision and Curriculum Development.

Peters, T. (1988). *Thriving on chaos.* New York: Alfred A. Knopf.

Sergiovanni, T.J. (1987). *The principalship: A reflective practice perspective.* Toronto: Allyn and Bacon, Inc.

Truscott, D.N. (1989). A model for strategic planning in a school. *The Canadian School Executive,* 9(4), 12-15.

Western Australia, Ministry of Education (1989). *School development plans: Policy and guidelines.* Perth, WA.

— (1990). *School decision-making: Policy and guidelines.* Perth, W.A.

# 3

# From Global To Local Environments

*It seems that rural people have to pay a heavy
social and economic price for living where they do.*

- a parent

There is great diversity among school-communities in sparsely populated areas. With such variation in mind, the purposes of this chapter are to describe some important features of many small school-community contexts and to emphasize the importance of contextual factors in strategic planning processes. To begin, imagine being a leader for schooling in these communities:

❖    ❖    ❖

*The Sheephorn community, a collection of ranches, is defined by a high mountain valley in Western Colorado with only a single access. Ranchers help each other out with spring branding before the cattle are herded out to summer range. Neighbors gather on Saturday night to visit and "share a bottle." The one-room school, which used to serve as the focus of the community, was closed in the late 50s during the last wave of consolidation, but some dimensions of "community" still remain.*

- from Noteworthy (1989) p. 3

*Norway House is an isolated community of 1 000 students located at the north end of Lake Winnipeg in Manitoba. The population is a mixture of native Indians, Metis and "southerners"*

*who have come north to work at the hydro station or in service in-
dustries. The three schools each feature a library and gymnasium
as well as special programs such as Cree, French, music and industrial arts. High school students and counsellors recently trav-
elled to another community to take part in a "Hug-in"—a drug
and alcohol prevention program founded in Minnesota. Goals for
the schools are excellence in instruction, increased parental involvement and marketing/public relations.*

- from Frontier, *Northerner,* August 1989

*Ejanding is in the heart of the Western Australian wheat and
sheep farming area. The community consists of six buildings and
a large wheat silo. The teacher's house is near the rail siding and
a sheep sheering shed. The families whose children attend the
school live on farms spread over 1 000 square kilometers. The primary school for ages of 4 to about 12 has 21 students, one teacher
and several part-time support staff. After grade 7 students are either bused to a district high school or attend a residential school
away from home. It is expected that everyone will co-operatively
encourage, maintain and participate in community activities including the school.*

- from *Rural Schools Within Their Communities*

*Morrin is a small, active community in west central Alberta. Ag-
riculture and oil are primary sources of income and also of major
importance is the nearby Royal Tyrell Museum which attracts
500 000 visitors annually. The community includes the usual
businesses and has several service clubs and recreation groups.
There is a growing number who belong to a Fundamentalist
church. The school for grades 1 to 12 has 198 students, 19 teachers and 4 support staff. It boasts a grade 12 completion rate of
90%. There are an increasing number of religious families who
are engaging in home schooling. While the school system has
quite a high level of participation among stakeholders and various ways of recognizing achievement and service, in a recent system review it was recommended that more attention be given to a
better integration of school and system initiatives and redefining
"the basics."*

- from *Starland System Planning Study*

❖    ❖    ❖

## The Changing Scene

It is beyond the purposes of this book to go into detail regarding various socio-political, economic and demographic changes taking place in non-urban areas. Those who live with these conditions day-by-day are well aware of the impact of declining population, economic hardship and the uncertainty of international market conditions for lumbering, mining, fishing, manufacturing and agriculture.

Recent papers for the National Conference of State Legislatures and the National Governors' Association reveal the nature of changes taking place in rural America (Nachtigal and Haas, 1988; Nachtigal and Hobbs, 1988). These writers point out that the percentage of Americans living in rural areas has dropped from about 60 percent to 30 percent since 1900 although actual numbers have been relatively constant at about 60 million. They also report that only one out of ten rural Americans is currently involved in farming. The decline in number of school districts according to Nachtigal and his associates is from 128 000 in 1930 to about 15 000 today. The startling point is that 55 percent of those districts enroll fewer than 600 students.

Developments and issues pertaining to rural America are receiving a good deal of national attention. Jones (1989), in reporting on the development of a new national rural policy, states "After a period of 'rural renaissance' in the 60s and 70s we are faced with the realization that rural America is losing jobs, losing business, losing people, and losing confidence" (p. 41). She goes on to say that developing effective leadership and decision-making capacity is at the heart of the problem of rural development.

There is a view among writers such as Nachtigal and Sher (1981) that the industrial age, driven by profit and the view that "bigger is better," has resulted in a level of centralization and standardization which has been destructive to rural America. They claim that the values noted above resulted in a "one best school system," top down approach to education which inevitably made rural schools "second best." They applaud efforts in states such as Missouri to remove the "urban bias," and initiatives toward community-based curriculum which build on the natural interdependence between schools and communities in isolated areas. Nachtigal believes further developments such as sustainable agriculture and natural farming, combined with a growing belief that there is "no one best answer," will support a renewal of some rural communities and schools. He also stresses the importance of schools and communities developing together.

Australia has always had major challenges in providing schooling in sparsely populated areas. At the time of the 1986 census 30 percent of Australia's 15.6 million people lived outside of major urban areas. Western Australia has only 1.3 million people in an area the size of Western Europe and over one million of those live in Perth. In the country as a whole, the small percentage of rural people provide over 80 percent of the exports. Attention to rural life is clearly in the national interest yet economic problems are very serious. During March, 1991, farmers in Western Australia dumped sheep carcasses on the steps of the legislature in Perth and another day they rented trucks to block freeways in order to pressure governments to do something about the low prices for wheat and wool.

The Federal (Commonwealth) Government in Australia recently adopted a strategy for rural education and training entitled "A Fair Go." It is to address concerns about rural students having lower grade 12 completion rates than urban students, access to education and training for all age groups, and opportunities for rural women, Aboriginals and ethnic groups. The Commonwealth Government has also sponsored a Country Areas Program which in 1989 gave 12.6 million dollars to schools for educational excursion programs, cultural enrichment, consultancy services, professional development, regional newspapers and teleconferences. Underlying this initiative was emphasis on community involvement.

In 1979 Perth, Western Australia, hosted a national conference on rural education. Subsequently the State Department of Education became involved in an OECD project and produced a series of monographs on rural education. One of these monographs identified problems in rural education related to diverse groups such as isolated families on stations 60 kilometres from the nearest neighbor, residents of settlements and minority ethnic communities. Isolation, uncertain commodity prices, lack of educational opportunities and disproportionate costs of schooling in rural areas were also considered problematic. Initiatives in the State to counter some of the difficulties include school transportation services, boarding schools, hostels, a correspondence school, Schools of the Air, an Isolated Students' Matriculation Scheme, a residential centre for children with learning difficulties and their parents, Aboriginal Schools, "Teaching Cottages" for upgrading and a Rural Integration Program for preschoolers. All schools in Western Australia are now required to involve parents and community in formulating annual School Development Plans.

Many of the trends in rural America and Australia apply to Canada. For example, The Canadian World Almanac, 1988, shows that the percentage of Canada's population considered rural has dropped from 62.5 percent in

1901 to 24.3 percent in 1981. Within the rural population, 66 percent were engaged in farming in 1931 compared to 17.6 percent in 1981. Again, we need to be reminded that at least four out of five rural people are not on farms.

The plight of the farm economy, fluctuations in oil prices, the impact of free trade on the lumber industry, problems in fishing and uncertainty in mining are well publicized in Canada. We hear of towns springing up and dying, of schools opening and closing, of "nest eggs" and subsidies but we have learned little about how to best provide schooling in such circumstances.

Canada suffers, in our opinion, from the absence of federal responsibility and initiative in education. In contrast to considerable attention at the national level in the United States and Australia, most efforts focused on education in sparsely populated areas of Canada have been within and by provinces. For example, in Saskatchewan in the early 1980s government, school trustees, teachers and universities worked together to do planning studies of rural jurisdictions which were experiencing severe enrolment decline (about 30 percent). The idea was to provide base-line data which school boards could use in scenario construction and long-range planning. This led to these same stakeholders co-operating to establish a provincial leadership centre, instruction centre and professional development centre to support rural school systems on a fee-for-service basis. In addition, the government had various studies and reports completed, established an educational development fund to encourage local initiative and built transportation, sparsity and small school factors into the foundation grant formula. As far as we know, similar developments took place in other provinces.

In summary, the scene in rural areas is changing dramatically and most trends can be described as "decline." Some attention has been given to problems which have surfaced regarding schooling in sparsely populated areas but it tends to reflect an urban bias and to be short-term. Hopes rest on changing values and improved leadership.

*Everything nowadays seems to be geared toward efficiency rather than quality. Just because a school with too few students in it isn't economical, government agencies believe in cutting costs by monopolizing the education system.*

- a parent

## Urban-Rural Differences

We often think of rural life as being slower paced and closer to nature. We have experienced the warmth of rural hospitality at the local rink, at a turkey supper, or in a big farm kitchen over home-baked cakes and several cups of coffee. We, no doubt, hold on to stereotypes of rural people "dropping in" for visits, of men wearing caps in restaurants and of personal "news" travelling quickly.

Urban-rural differences should be kept in mind if we are to redesign schools effectively. Paul Nachtigal has offered the comparison shown in Table 3.1. He stresses, too, that characteristics should be seen on a continuum and that rural communities vary greatly. According to him, degrees of "ruralness" depend upon economic resources, cultural priorities, commonality of purpose, political efficacy, size and isolation. How do these differences compare to your views? What would you add to or delete from the list?

### Table 3.1 Rural-Urban Differences

| Rural | Urban |
| --- | --- |
| personal/tightly linked | impersonal/loose |
| generalists | specialists |
| homogeneous | heterogeneous |
| nonbureaucratic | bureaucratic |
| verbal communication | written communication |
| who said it | what was said |
| time measured by seasons | time by the clock/calendar |
| traditional values | liberal values |
| entrepreneur ~specialty~or~ | corporate persons  ~big business~ |
| "make do" response to environment | rational planning to control environment |
| self-sufficiency | leave problem solving to experts |
| less disposable income | more disposable income |
| less formal education | more formal education |
| smaller | larger |
| low population density | higher population density |
| acquaintances: fewer, diverse in age/culture | acquaintances: many, similar to self |
| school: to preserve local culture/community | school: to get ahead in the world |
| teachers: central to community | teachers: separate from community |
| students: known by everyone | students: known by teachers and friends |

adapted from Paul Nachtigal, *Rural Education: In Search of a Better Way*, (1982), p. 270.

Some attention in the literature has been given to a comparison of rural and urban schools. Difficulties commonly associated with rural schools include limited resources, restricted curriculum, shortage of specialist teachers, fewer opportunities for professional development and the difficulties in dealing with local politics. One principal told us recently, for example, that five local women had applied for one teacher aide position and, no matter how he decided, the four not hired would be "on his case." Rural schools are generally considered to have advantages related to lower pupil-teacher ratios, closer working relationships, a spirit of sharing, a greater proportion of students involved in co-curricular programs and leadership activities, lower cost of living and slower pace of living. Many of these factors combine in some regions to result in lower drop-out rates for rural schools than for urban schools. The fall, 1990, *Newsletter* of the Canadian Education Association indicates that larger communities were more likely to give schools an "F" (failing grade) and that urban areas were twice as likely as rural areas to cite lack of discipline as a problem in schools. There is some evidence that rural teachers derive satisfaction primarily from the people with them day-by-day in the school-community whereas urban teachers are more impressed by good facilities, opportunities for personal and professional growth and administrative support.

The question of quality of education is receiving increased attention in response to societal pressure for accountability, economic problems and the possibility of further consolidation of rural schools. A leading authority in the United States, Jonathan Sher (1988) claims that "there is no compelling evidence that larger schools provide either a better education or cost savings to the state or district." A 1985 review of provincial diploma test results in Alberta showed that students in schools of fewer than 200 had results above the provincial norm in three subjects, below the average in three and equal to the average in one. Our experience supports the position that students from small schools do just as well, on average, on standardized tests in academic subjects as students from urban schools. We hasten to add two points, however: there is great variation among small schools and one challenge presented in this book is to make all schools as effective as the best; there is growing concern about heavy reliance on standardized tests. There are many initiatives to make student evaluation more broadly-based in keeping with the general goal of preparing students for lifelong learning. The state of Missouri, Western Australia and the province of Alberta are three leaders in developing student centred, performance indicators using quantitative and qualitative data to measure growth in knowledge, attitudes and skills. In our opinion, rural leaders should strongly support this work since it will help to remove urban bias in traditional student evaluation practices. It would also enable everyone to see whether or not potential advantages of "smallness" in relation to areas such as integrated curriculum, independent learning and self concept are being realized.

People who have lived in both urban and rural school-communities know that there are differences between them. They have lived and felt the differences either with satisfaction or dissatisfaction. We must surface the differences, talk about them and consider how they may affect efforts to redesign schools.

> *I enjoy it here. I really, really do. I don't plan on*
> *moving for a few years simply because I enjoy it.*
> - a beginning teacher

## The Challenge

Schools and communities in sparsely populated areas are interwoven and interdependent. Neither can go far without the other so leaders for schooling have to give increased attention to the local context if the potential advantages of small schools are to be realized.

There are some success stories. After a case study of five communities, Wall and Luther at the Heartland Center for Leadership Development, State of Nebraska, set forth 20 clues to rural community survival. Examination of their list in Table 2.2 underlines the importance of a future orientation, participation, integration, information, competitive positioning, wise use of fiscal resources, networks and revitalized leadership— many components of strategic planning. How does their list compare to your experience? The points to be emphasized are that school leaders need to become community leaders and that contextual factors are powerful.

There are choices and some shining examples of development, yet leaders everywhere, whether in business, industry, government or education, are facing tremendous challenges. Bennis (1990) in his book, *Why Leaders Can't Lead*, cited isolation, cynicism, routine, inertia and turmoil as reasons for lack of leadership. After discovering that 61 percent of principals and vice-principals felt less effective than they did five years ago, Fullan (1988), entitled his book *What's Worth Fighting for in the Principalship?* We may ask "What's worth fighting for in rural education?" We believe the quick answer is "students." Beyond that, the challenge is not to get overwhelmed with the problems and complexities of rural contexts but to build upon their unique features to provide community education for learners of all ages—a community of learners.

### Table 3.2 Twenty Clues to Rural Community Survival

1. Evidence of community pride
2. Emphasis on quality in business and community life
3. Willingness to invest in the future
4. Participatory approach to community decision making
5. Co-operative community spirit
6. Realistic appraisal of future opportunities
7. Awareness of competitive positioning
8. Knowledge of physical environment
9. Active economic development program
10. Deliberate transition of power to a younger generation of leaders
11. Acceptance of women in leadership roles
12. Strong belief in and support for education
13. Problem-solving approach to providing health care
14. Strong multi-generational family orientation
15. Strong presence of traditional institutions that are integral to community life
16. Attention to sound and well-maintained infrastructure
17. Careful use of fiscal resources
18. Sophisticated use of information resources
19. Willingness to seek help from the outside
20. Conviction that, in the long run, you have to do it yourself

Source: Heartland Center for Leadership Development, Lincoln, Nebraska.

> We believe a strategic planning process which includes a thorough scan of the local community environment offers the best hope of redesigning and revitalizing small schools. The first step is to listen to the people to learn about their beliefs, values and understanding in relation to schooling.

There are many examples of leaders for schooling integrating their efforts with those of people in industry and business. The developments reported below, and others readers will be able to think of, illustrate that small schools can be special!

## Turning to Illustrations

In the gold-mining area of Western Australia a mining company provides tree seedlings and soil to schools. The students grow the seedlings and then sell them back to the company!

In Yerecoin, Western Australia, primary school students buy sheep and grow vegetables in order to provide meaningful learning experiences and some profit.

After conducting a housing survey, some students in Custer, South Dakota and their teacher were invited to join the Chamber of Commerce where they continue to serve on standing committees.

In Spruce Grove, Alberta, a hydroponics food company is training high school students to work in the labs so that they may be prepared for future employment in the Arctic.

*Teaching staff should be screened as to familiarity with rural life, where there is a different attitude and way of life than in urban areas.*

- a teacher

# References

Alberta Education (1985). *Student achievement: small schools versus the province.* Paper presented at the Manitoba Small School Symposium, Morris and Morden, September.

Bennis, W. (1990). *Why leaders can't lead: The unconscious conspiracy continues.* San Francisco: Jossey-Bass.

Frontier School Division (1989). *Drug abuse programs.* School Division Newsletter, Winnipeg, Manitoba, August.

Fullan, M. (1988). *What's worth fighting for in the principalship?* Toronto: Ontario Public School Teachers' Federation.

Jones, S.H. (Ed.) (1989). *Options in developing a new national rural policy: Rural policy development workshops.* Texas A & M University.

Mid-continent Regional Educational Laboratory (1989). Rural communities and their schools: Creating a more promising future. *Noteworthy,* Rural Institute. Aurora: Colorado.

Nachtigal, P. (1982). *Rural education: In search of a better way.* Boulder, CA: Westview Press.

Nachtigal, P. & Haas, T. (1988). *The new school finance research agenda: Resource utilization in schools and school districts restructuring rural schools.* A paper prepared for the National Conference of State Legislatures. McREL, Aurora, Colorado, May.

Nachtigal, P. & Hobbs, D. (1988). *Rural development: The role of the public schools.* Background paper, National Governors' Association, June.

Sher, J. (Ed.) (1981). *Rural education in urbanized nations.* An OECD/CERI report. Boulder, Colorado: Westview Press.

Wall, M. & Luther, V. (1987). *20 clues to rural community survival: A community case study project.* Lincoln, Nebraska: Heartland Center for Leadership Development.

Western Australia Education Department (1980). *Rural schools within their communities.* Studies in rural education No. 4, Perth, WA: Research Branch.

# SECTION TWO

# Voices

In this section the voices of students, parents, community, teachers and principals are featured. In each chapter we have attempted to connect the "big picture" with developments "closer to home." As well, each chapter is organized under the headings of thinking, relating, planning and thinking again. In this way readers are invited to engage in continuous learning cycles and to make connections among our thoughts, their ideas and local contexts. In the strategic planning process, the voices form the basis of internal analysis—what is going on in the schools day-by-day from a variety of perspectives?

# 4

- Student miss/rep
- written survey
- letters

# The Voice of Students

*We barely ever get a say in much. They have
a survey but nothing ever comes of it.*

- a student

Schools are for students. Government documents say they should be. More and more emphasis in provinces and states is on *student* outcomes. Models for school improvement place the student at the centre. All of this is reinforced by lessons from businesses that successful companies "focus on the customer." Individual attention is frequently cited by students, parents and teachers as a special strength of schools in sparsely populated areas, and in some of these schools drop-out rates are lower than in urban schools. At the same time, surveys indicate that student voice in school decisions is the low point of school climate profiles and this is most pronounced among senior students. Representatives of Future Farmers of America recently made a plea for improved two-way communication and increased respect between young people and school-community leaders. A sophisticated view was shared by a senior student in rural Saskatchewan who said, "I would change school policy to ensure that things would be more fair and that decisions would be more broad-minded—based on the good of the school, not personal beliefs."

Data for this chapter are drawn primarily from planning studies which included 938 questionnaires from students, all of which had written comments to open questions. In addition, 20 school system reviews from the province of Alberta have been summarized and recent developments in schools of the central region of the United States have been noted.

# Thinking

## *The Big Picture*

Many environmental factors, particularly global economic conditions, immigration policies, emphasis on human capital and the public push for accountability focus attention on students. Some happy events such as exchange programs, student involvement in the community and co-curricular activities are reported regularly in the media but issues related to drugs, alcohol, sex and violence in schools clearly dominate the news. In small communities adults shake their heads at the way young people behave on weekends. One student reported, "A party isn't a social gathering, it's getting totally blitzed so you don't even remember last Friday." The view of the authors is that we need to highlight "good news" of student leadership in schools and in communities. Readers will be able to think of students collecting money for UNICEF, putting on a Christmas party for the needy, initiating a safe-grad program, and contributing in many ways to quality of life and learning at school. We have all noted that many societal forces are weighing on young people at the same time as public expectations increase. Youth need supporters, mentors and advocates—a central role for school administrators and elected officials.

Despite "lip service" to student-centred schooling and the advantages of low pupil-teacher ratios in many small schools, our experience indicates that effective involvement of students is not common. System evaluations in Alberta typically reveal student perceptions of a "lack of say" in matters that affect them. Fewer than half of grade 7–12 students in Saskatchewan surveys feel involved in decisions about life at school. Schmuck and Schmuck (1990) found a general lack of participation in decision making in small schools of America. A student panelist at a recent retreat of Alberta administrators and Ministry personnel remarked, "They are not as tolerant of personal views in high school as they are at university. You got better marks if you expressed the teacher's views—you were doing things for others." This comment adds the dimension of student voice in classroom learning as well as in decision making about schooling.

No doubt many realities make it difficult to hear student voices about schooling. Schools are hierarchical in relation to authority and curriculum. Our tradition is clearly "top down." It is also more comfortable and safer for teachers and administrators when they are "in charge." More student voice would make schools and classrooms less predictable. Professional educators would need to share leadership and control. How ready are we for that? How can provincial/state requirements be reconciled with increased attention to student voice? Before pursuing these questions further we need to look more closely at some student views.

### Closer to Home

In this, and other chapters in this Section, actual data from a recent survey of a rural jurisdiction in Saskatchewan are shared. The purpose of such reporting is to provide a mirror from which you may reflect on the situation in your schools (reflection requires something against which perceptions may be considered) and to give practical examples of how data may be collected. To assist with the interpretation of the data the context of the school system will be briefly described.

Big Valley School Division is a combination of rolling hills and flat farmland in southern Saskatchewan. The "big valley," used as a community pasture, separates the area into three schools in the east and five in the west including three in the main town of 3 000 people. In addition there is a small K-4 school in the south and one school in a Hutterite colony. Because of the large valley in the middle of the area, most schools are near the boundary of neighboring school systems. The East schools, for example, are much closer to a city of 35 000 to the north than they are to Maintown. In 1946 and in 1964 school enrolment was 2 214 and 2 330 respectively. Current grades and enrolments are shown in Table 4.1.

### Table 4.1 Schools in the Big Valley School Division 1990

| School | | | Grades | Students | Teachers (FTE) |
|---|---|---|---|---|---|
| East A | | | K-12 | 60 | 7 |
| B | | | K-12 | 54 | 5 |
| C | | | K-12 | 39 | 4 |
| West D | | | K-12 | 200 | 14 |
| E | | | K-12 | 119 | 8 |
| Maintown | F | | K-2 | 184 | 8 |
| | G | | 3-8 | 346 | 21 |
| | H | | 9-12 | 207 | 12 |
| Other I | | | K-4 | 15 | 1 |
| Hutterite J | | | K-8 | 15 | 1 |
| | | | | 1 239 | 81 |

Although several issues prompted the board of the Big Valley S.D. to contract for a planning study, the central one had to do with small schools. School A had a capacity for 200 students but parents in communities B and

C had refused to send even their older children there. The board had set a policy to close school "I" but the picketing of the board chairman's grocery store in Maintown and the marriage of his daughter to one of the "local boys" prevented that. Community E is only 10 minutes from Maintown but parents refuse to send high school students there even though facilities are available for Home Economics and Industrial Arts. One parent commented, "My truck is eight years old and it never has made a right turn at the junction to go to Maintown." Underlying these issues were the continuing economic hardship and concern about the quality of education in small schools. The budget of 5.4 million dollars was provided by an almost equal contribution from local taxes and provincial grants. Per pupil expenditures of $4,137 were about average for rural divisions in the province.

Leadership and political influence were two additional crucial considerations in the Big Valley S.D. Each school, in accordance with provincial legislation, had an elected local board of trustees to act in an advisory role to the board of education for the school division. There were 54 local board members and 7 system board members in 1990. Only the superintendent was in a leadership position without teaching responsibilities.

The description of the context of the Big Valley S.D. will enable readers to better interpret specific data which follow and to determine the extent to which they may apply to school systems in which they work and live.

**Student Views of Program.** In an effort to focus on students in the Big Valley S.D., student representatives were interviewed in phase one of the study in order to formulate items for questionnaires. Later every student K-12 responded in class to a questionnaire. Items were categorized under program, climate and life outside of school although it was recognized that family, community and school life do come together in some fashion for each student.

Kindergarten to grade 3 students indicated that they enjoy school—the work, other students and the teachers. Approximately 90 percent of the responses were positive in these areas. They also understand the expectations to do well and to be neat. The lowest items (with 50-60 percent positive answers) were related to student behaviour at recess, parents talking to teachers and the bus ride to and from school.

At least four out of five grade 4 to 6 students had positive views of themselves, teacher and parent expectations, help from the teacher, following rules and fun at recess. In contrast fewer than one-half were positive about school in general, teacher caring, praise from principal, student behavior at recess and noon, parents coming to the school and parents talking to the teacher. The diversity of views and the interest of students in responding clearly indicates that they are more than passive participants in the learning process.

Grade 7 to 12 student views are reported in some detail in Tables 4.2 and 4.3. It can be seen that the items with the highest positive percentages are related to extra-curricular activities, the amount of learning taking place, opportunities for success in class and class size. This would likely be interpreted as good news by most leaders. The greatest number of negative perceptions centred around counselling, second languages and course options. It should be noted that concerns about counselling and course options are typical of both Saskatchewan and Alberta surveys. These results, of course, are only a starting point for clarification, discussion and planning with students and other stakeholders.

### Table 4.2 Students' Views of School Program (N = 366)

| Program Component | Percentage of responses | | |
|---|---|---|---|
| | Positive | Neutral | Negative |
| 1. The number of course options | 42.6 | 16.2 | 41.2[1] |
| 2. Emphasis on basic skills | 77.0 | 15.3 | 7.7 |
| 3. Homework: fair, satisfactory | 51.9 | 22.8 | 25.2 |
| 4. How much you are learning | 73.3 | 13.6 | 13.0 |
| 5. The marks assigned to you | 64.4 | 17.4 | 17.8 |
| 6. What is reported to your parents | 61.0 | 22.1 | 16.8 |
| 7. Extra-curricular activities | 81.0 | 9.9 | 9.2 |
| 8. Student representative council | 69.6 | 16.6 | 13.8 |
| 9. The school facility | 63.5 | 26.2 | 11.3 |
| 10. Chances for success in class | 72.9 | 16.0 | 11.0 |
| 11. The length of class periods | 58.5 | 19.2 | 22.2 |
| 12. Rewards available | 50.4 | 22.6 | 27.0 |
| 13. The number of students per class | 72.1 | 10.1 | 17.9 |
| 14. Resources in the library | 53.0 | 22.0 | 25.0 |
| 15. Second language program | 32.5 | 23.3 | 44.2 |
| 16. Usefulness of courses | 60.1 | 22.1 | 17.8 |
| 17. Availability of a counsellor | 22.5 | 22.2 | 55.4 |

[1] Percentage may not total 100 because of rounding off and blank responses.

Closely related to general views of program are student voices pertaining to various subject areas. It is clear that a majority of students want more emphasis in the future on career education, physical education, counselling and computer related programs. It is interesting to note how close these are to environmental factors having to do with employment, health and technology. Relatively high numbers want more emphasis on art, music and drama and so seem to lend support to what Naisbitt and Aburdene (1990) call a "renaissance in the arts" as one of 10 trends for this decade. In many ways students are on the "cutting edge" of social issues and developments. Our experience suggests that they may be ahead of the adults.

### Table 4.3 Students' Views of Program Emphasis for the Future (N = 366)

| Program Component | Percentage of responses | | |
|---|---|---|---|
| | Less | Same | More |
| 1. Art | 11.5 | 43.7 | 44.8[1] |
| 2. French | 43.5 | 29.1 | 27.4 |
| 3. Health | 7.1 | 66.8 | 26.0 |
| 4. English | 15.3 | 67.7 | 17.0 |
| 5. Mathematics | 13.4 | 62.6 | 24.0 |
| 6. Physical Education | 4.4 | 35.9 | 59.7 |
| 7. Music | 34.4 | 33.3 | 32.2 |
| 8. Science | 11.8 | 70.7 | 17.5 |
| 9. Social Studies | 25.3 | 62.6 | 12.4 |
| 10. Industrial Arts | 10.2 | 46.3 | 43.5 |
| 11. Home Economics | 16.6 | 43.4 | 39.9 |
| 12. Career Education | 5.7 | 30.6 | 63.7 |
| 13. Guidance Counselling | 12.9 | 34.6 | 52.6 |
| 14. Drama | 12.8 | 45.8 | 41.4 |
| 15. Computer Education | 11.3 | 37.7 | 51.0 |
| 16. Accounting | 14.9 | 42.7 | 42.4 |
| 17. Law | 13.1 | 38.6 | 48.3 |
| 18. Band | 45.0 | 35.5 | 19.5 |

[1] Percentages may not total 100 because of rounding off and blank responses.

**Student Views of School Climate**. Characteristics of effective schools as well as our own experience highlight the importance of school climate. Students' views from a school climate survey are summarized in Table 4.4. The general pattern for all schools is primarily positive (at least 80 percent) in terms of the interest of parents, teachers' expectations, teachers' knowledge of subject matter, teacher preparation and students' desire to do well. It seems fair to say student reactions are "mixed" in relation to teachers taking a personal interest in students, teachers being in class on time, the nature of rules/regulations, the presence of school spirit, care of school property, decor, student behavior in class and student voice in decisions. While the pattern revealed in Table 4.4 is typical of many jurisdictions in which we have worked, there is important variation from school to school even within the same school system. For example, the percentage of positive responses to school spirit ranged from a low of 18 percent in one school to a high of 64 percent in another. Moreover, the climate profiles do not appear to be related to school size—small schools are not always "one happy family".

**General Views**. According to our surveys, typical high school students would give the school a "C." They have concerns about too few course options and inadequate career counselling. Most would prefer to remain in their small school rather than ride the bus farther to a larger school. They consider high marks important and do one-half to one hour of homework each school night. Activities in order of importance are sports, homework, meeting other students, work outside of school, watching television and community service. Typical comments include:

*Our school is so small that it really isn't worth it to be putting a lot of time and money into it.*

*I would like to change the number of subjects to give a student a better opportunity in the 'real' world.*

*We rely a lot on correspondence. Most of us get better marks in correspondence than at our school.*

*I like a smaller school because you are not just a face in the crowd.*

### Table 4.4 Students' Views - Selected Items
### from a School Climate Survey (N = 366)

| Item | Percentage of responses | | |
|------|:--------:|:-------:|:--------:|
| | **Positive** | **Neutral** | **Negative** |
| 1. I enjoy school | 52.8 | 27.6 | 19.7[1] |
| 2. Students get along well | 72.9 | 13.7 | 13.4 |
| 3. Teachers take a personal interest in me | 37.9 | 36.5 | 25.6 |
| 4. Teachers are available to give extra help | 72.3 | 14.3 | 13.5 |
| 5. Teachers know the subject matter | 86.3 | 7.8 | 5.9 |
| 6. Teachers are enthusiastic about teaching | 57.7 | 30.9 | 11.3 |
| 7. Teachers are in class on time | 42.5 | 26.5 | 30.9 |
| 8. Teachers are prepared | 81.3 | 13.5 | 5.2 |
| 9. Teachers expect me to do my best | 94.7 | 4.4 | 0.8 |
| 10. School rules and regulations are fair | 50.4 | 21.5 | 28.1 |
| 11. There is a good school spirit | 34.2 | 23.6 | 42.2 |
| 12. Students take care of school property | 36.0 | 26.4 | 37.6 |
| 13. School is a good place to make friends | 71.6 | 16.0 | 12.4 |
| 14. I like to do well in school | 80.4 | 6.8 | 2.7 |
| 15. My parents are interested in how I do | 94.8 | 3.6 | 1.6 |
| 16. Students willingly participate | 50.1 | 25.1 | 24.8 |
| 17. Discipline is firm and consistent | 59.2 | 22.5 | 16.3 |
| 18. There is good teacher-student co-operation | 52.0 | 28.3 | 19.7 |
| 19. Our school is well decorated | 42.2 | 25.2 | 32.6 |
| 20. The principal does a good job | 67.0 | 9.8 | 23.2 |
| 21. We have an adequate say in decisions that affect us | 39.0 | 23.4 | 37.6 |
| 22. Students behave well in class | 30.7 | 35.9 | 33.5 |

[1] Percentages may not total 100 because of rounding off and blank responses.

There is an interesting difference in many communities in student and parent voices about school closure. In one community, for example, 92 percent of the parents oppose closure and 61 percent of the grade 7–12 students would prefer a larger school.

Alberta data indicate that parents are the most satisfied of all stakeholders in schooling, the teachers are second and students are least satisfied. The realization that 30 to 40 percent of the high school students leave before completing senior matriculation adds some urgency to listening to student voices about schooling.

## Turning to Illustrations

Having students at the centre of a school system requires a focus on students at every level from the classroom to the board table, and in all aspects of schooling from learning and instruction to management. A focus on students is not easy to maintain, however, as there tends to be a shift to subject content emphasis in higher grades and to political considerations at the board table. In addition, teacher resource manuals and curriculum guides have traditionally stressed what teachers should do, not what students could do. The authors take the position that student voice in selection of content, strategies for learning and assessment are vital to relevance of schooling. We believe that putting students first will eventually result in political gains but risk taking is inevitable. For example, imagine a superintendent who insists that an expelled student needs to be given another chance against the wishes of the principal, or a board which passes a motion to adopt a health program despite warnings that some parents will not approve. There is still a belief that letting students get out of their desks creates uncertainty and risk yet there is increasing support for the concept of "schools without walls" and schools in the community for specific learning experiences. The Alberta School Act defines a school not as a building, but as a structured learning environment. Many developments reflect risk taking and strong leadership.

In communities all across the United States young people are leaving school to conduct surveys, to register voters, to clean up neighborhoods, to visit nursing homes and to educate children about drugs. To these students and to the teachers who are involved, school is not only a place to learn but also an important community resource. The states of Maryland and Minnesota require schools to offer formal opportunities for students to become involved in community service. It was stated at a 1990 International Rural and Small Schools Conference in Bismarck, North Dakota that "everybody wins" when rural young people can earn high school credit for community service (students develop new commitment, there is new relevance for the curriculum and new vitality for small communities).

More than 50 students in Red Deer, Alberta, have formed a group known as STOP (Students and Teachers Opposing Prejudice). It all started when a creative teacher, Darren Lund, read students a poem he had written about society's apathy to racism. The group meets after school to "start making a difference." They have received a grant from Multiculturalism and Citizenship Canada to assist in producing a STOP magazine which has been distributed to every school in the province. They have raised money to sponsor a Honduran foster child, written letters to win the release of political prisoners and held province-wide poetry and poster contests.

"The Rural Science and North High School Without Walls" is a new project designed to address lack of student interest in, and availability of, senior math and science courses in rural schools in South Dakota. Through a consortium of rural high schools, the University of South Dakota, the State Education Agency, the Midcontinent Regional Education Laboratory (McREL) and the Annenberg/CPB project (to provide high quality education electronically) the project began in the summer of 1990. Rural teachers had a four-week institute on campus where faculty assisted in their preparation for the courses and for two of the weeks teachers were joined by teams of students from their schools who would serve as teaching/networking assistants during the school year. The project is underway in 23 schools all networked into the University computer system.

The Missouri State Board of Education has made a long-term commitment through a State School Improvement Program to be student-focused. Their document, July 1990 is entitled "Missourians Prepared—Success for Every Student." The comprehensive plan highlights increasing time for teaching and learning, alternatives and flexibility for students, equity and opportunity, a Parents as Teachers program, recruitment and professional development of teachers and related financial support. Student views are an integral part of monitoring, reporting, and planning for school improvement. Schools are then classified as "approved," "probation" or "unapproved." One major aim is to remove an anti-rural bias (bigger is better) in earlier classification schemes.

## Relating

The reading up to this point and the related thinking has been an individual effort. The purpose of this section is to extend our thoughts by language and by dialogue. Dialogue, as compared to discussion, requires active listening and suspending our beliefs about "what is" and "what might be." Particularly in relation to students we need to be reminded to concentrate on trends and issues more than on events. A championship team or an alcohol-related accident should not keep us from looking at the "bigger picture" in relation to athletics in schooling and substance abuse among students. The following questions may assist in relating to students and to colleagues about the voice of students in schooling:

1. What are the "big picture" or societal factors that are having the greatest impact on students in your school system? Some considerations are part-time jobs, prospects for careers, environmental issues, pregnancies and substance abuse.

2. What are the trends or issues in student achievement, dropouts, vandalism, the co-curricular program, and community partnership?

3. Do students feel they have a voice in decisions which affect their schooling?

4. How are students involved in the community at the present time? Do they participate in recreational, religious and cultural activities? Do many have part-time jobs? How does what they are learning there relate to the school program?

5. What leadership are students offering at home, in the community and at school? Do they feel respected and supported in initiatives they may wish to take?

6. How important is increased student voice and involvement to improved learning opportunities for individuals and for school-community development? How important is it to me as a leader?

7. Are there ways in which student voices could be made more influential in our school system?

> *My child learned that the big guy with the backing of*
> *the school board was more important than a kid. The*
> *children simply had virtually no one on their side.*
>
> - a parent

## Planning

The challenge at this stage is to be an active learner. Considering the thoughts that crossed your mind in reading the first section of this chapter, and the results of relating your ideas with others, what further directions need to be taken? The guidelines below are based upon our understanding of related literature and our experience in working with leaders of schooling in sparsely populated areas. We have thought of leaders who are just at the stage of initiating activity in this area as well as those who are at stages of redesigning.

## Initiating

If you have not paid much attention to students' voices in schooling, you likely want to further prepare yourself by doing more reading, making more observations and continuing dialogue with partners at the system level. You may want to review data already available in your school system pertaining to achievement levels, drop-out rates, student union activities, students' choice of courses and cases of student-teacher conflict. At the same time, you could begin to clarify your ideas of "what should be." All of the planning above is low profile and personal to form the basis for a public position that you wish to take. If the gap between what you believe to be going on and the best that you can imagine is narrow you may simply commend all those involved and use the results in the strategic planning process. On the other hand, if the gap in your opinion is wide enough to require action on your part it is time to decide what time and energy you need to devote to it. The importance of a personal position cannot be overemphasized as it is the foundation of trust. Only when people know where leaders stand on important issues, in this instance student voice, do they feel that leaders can be trusted.

We hope that we are at the point where a superintendent or board member can take a position regarding students' involvement in the school system and share it at a principals' meeting or a board meeting. This action is relating at the organizational level. Depending upon your views and those of others, plans could be made to provide more opportunities for students' voices to be heard. A logical first step would be to ask principals for ideas and participation. This could result in interviews with student leaders, a determination of trends and/or the administration of a student questionnaire.

Very few would oppose listening more carefully to what students have to say about schooling and it is relatively easy and inexpensive to do so. The difficult part is to follow up the listening with related action. The action could be threatening to some staff members and could "stir up" the community. It could also be expensive. We have seen student data earlier in this chapter that strongly suggests the hiring of a guidance counsellor. That same data reveal very low ratings for one particular principal. In other words, we are asking for trouble if we solicit student views and don't follow through. We need to see how the student voices will be utilized in the strategic planning process for the school system and make that known at the outset.

## Redesigning

If student data have already been systematically collected in your school system the challenge, as noted above, is to use that information in the strategic planning processes. If issues have changed or if new trends have surfaced, new information will have to be obtained. This may mean a second administration of a questionnaire, a year or two after the first, to examine trends and issues. For example, the survey of students in the Big Valley School Division confirms the usual attributes of small schools including close personal relations within the school and community. Several students in interviews and through comments claim, however, that this is a disadvantage since, if a student has a negative image, there is no escape. One student said, "Teachers know you too well." From another school a student stated, "The community shouldn't use the school for discipline for after-school or weekend happenings." Gjelton, in writing of the New Haven Project, found that the school had to be a refuge for students—a neutral place where they could escape the community role/reputation laid on them. School as refuge is, no doubt, a sensitive, redesign issue!

Further sophistication can take place once base-line data from students are established. It is a mistake to collect more information than will be utilized as people will expect related action. Student school climate surveys are not usually necessary every year. Questionnaires are not the most effective way to hear the voices of students. An annual luncheon meeting with student representatives would likely pay big dividends for superintendents and board members. One superintendent with whom we work has regular "think tanks" with students.

The challenge for leaders in the redesign of ways to hear student voices is to maintain a balance of pressure and support for the process. Let it be known that you expect students to always be respected and heard both formally and informally. Do not let listening to student voices be a "one-shot" or annual event. Support the process with time, money and professional development for staff. Students need time to talk to teachers, to principals and to superintendents. A common complaint from students is that there is no such time—they are either in class or on the bus and at noon teachers are at lunch. Senior students continually make a plea for some space at school to, more or less, call their own. Teachers, especially in K-12 schools, need continuous support in improving classroom and hallway interaction with students. On a questionnaire a husky, grade 11, male student wrote, "I just wish she would quit saying 'Now settle down kiddies'."

A crucial part of maintaining support for, and interest in, student involvement in schooling is to monitor trends and results. (More attention will be given to monitoring in a later chapter.) This may be relatively simple, such as noting how many girls enrol in senior science courses or seeing if alcohol awareness programs change drinking habits. The results, however, must be on paper—"gut reactions" and general impressions will not be convincing enough for redesign initiatives or for the publics' expectations for accountability. Have you planned for monitoring?

Student voice will assuredly lead to change and changes in schools inevitably disquiet adults somewhat. Debra Schroeder puts forth a personal challenge:

### I'm Ready, Are You?

*I'm ready to live*
*Ready to grow*
*Ready for all the love you show.*
*Ready for laughter—*
*Ready for fun—*
*Ready for life that's just begun.*
*Ready for touching*
*Ready to talk*
*Ready to crawl and climb and walk.*
*Ready for friends*
*Ready to play*
*Ready for new things everyday.*
*Ready to learn*
*Ready to know*
*Ready for school where I must go.*

*Are you ready for me?*
*Ready to see —*
*All the things that I can be?*
*Ready to meet me*
*Where I am?*
*Ready to teach me what you can?*
*Ready to guide?*

*Ready to lead?*
*Ready to help me to succeed?*
*Ready to challenge?*
*Ready to change?*
*Ready your world to rearrange?*

*I'm ready today—ready to do*
*So many things if you'll help me to.*
*Teacher, the time has come when you—*
*Must answer the question, "Are You Ready Too?"*

- Debra Schroeder

## Thinking Again

Writing this chapter has changed our beliefs and thoughts about "student voice" related to schooling. We are convinced that with all our many responsibilities we often neglect what schooling is all about—student voices which are closely related to student learning. During the past few months as we continue to work in small schools we have been struck by how often opportunities for dialogue with students are missed. One very positive feature of these schools is "smallness" which should be conducive to rich, continuing dialogue among students, staff and other adults in the community. We must think of better ways to hear those student voices as a starting point for the redesign and revitalization of small schools.

*Policies that the school obtains are not consistent.*
*Parents are not told the policies and neither are the students.*
*I, as a student, would like to be told what is going on with my school.*

- a student

# References

Alberta Education (1988). County *System Review*. Calgary Regional Office, 1200 Rocky Mt. Plaza, 615 Macleod Trail, S.E., Calgary, Alberta, T2G 4T8.

Alberta Education (1989). *System Review*. Calgary Regional Office, 1200 Rocky Mt. Plaza, 615 Macleod Trail, S.E., Calgary, Alberta, T2G 4T8.

Alberta Education (1985). *System Study*. Calgary Regional Office, 1200 Rocky Mt. Plaza, 615 Macleod Trial, S.E., Calgary, Alberta, T2G 4T8.

Canada Multiculturalism and Citizenship (1990). Red Deer students promote understanding. *Together* (i),4,11.

Conrad, D. & Hedin, D. (1989). *High school community service: A review of research and programs*. Unpublished manuscript. National Center on Effective Secondary Schools, University of Wisconsin, Madison, Wisconsin, 53706.

Gjelton, T. (1978). *Schooling in isolated communities*. Portland, Maine 04112, Box 13: North Haven Project for Career Development.

Mid-continent Regional Educational Laboratory (1990). *The rural science and math high school without walls*. Aurora, Colorado, 12500, E. Iliff Avenue, 201, 80014.

Missouri State Board of Education (1990). *Missourians prepared—success for every student*. Jefferson City, Missouri, P.O. Box 480, 65102.

Naisbitt, J. & Aburdene, P. (1990). *Megatrends 2000: Ten new directions for the 1990's*. New York: Avon Books.

Saskatchewan Educational Leadership Unit (1988). *Directions for the 1990's* (A planning study of a rural school division). University of Saskatchewan, Saskatoon, Saskatchewan, S7N 0W0.

Saskatchewan Educational Leadership Unit (1990). *Planning for the 1990's* (A study of a rural school division). Saskatchewan, Saskatoon.

Schmuck, P. & Schmuck, R. (1990). *Democratic participation in small-town schools*. Paper presented at the annual meeting of the National Rural Education Association, October, Colorado Springs.

**5**

# The Voice of Parents and Community

*They want you to come but they don't listen.*

- a parent

Increasingly popular topics among leaders in education are "Parents as Partners," "Parents as First Teachers," "Marketing Your Schools" and "Rural Schools and Community Development." Not only is increased involvement of parents and community in schools being advocated, it is intuitively appealing—it seems to make sense. It would also seem that such involvement could be more easily attained in sparsely populated areas than in urban contexts. Close working relationships with parents and community are, indeed, areas of excellence in some small schools yet, as the title of this book suggests, in many contexts parents feel they have little voice. After visits to 24 school districts in 21 states, Schmuck and Schmuck (1990) concluded that there was an absence of collaboration and co-operation in small town schools.

Data for this chapter are drawn primarily from two sources. There are planning studies which included 1 012 parent questionnaires and we have included relevant data from system studies in Alberta. Interviews and "town hall" meetings also provided information. Frequent reference is also made to the Frontier School Division in northern Manitoba where for some time parental-community involvement has been a priority.

## Thinking

*The Big Picture*

The involvement of parents and community in schooling can be considered from many perspectives. Historically, we have read reports of education (as compared to the narrower term "schooling") in ancient Greece and among native people of this continent. Many tales are told of one-room schools in communities early in this century. Today we hear of mothers in Japan attending classes when children are sick so that "nothing is missed." From a sociological perspective, we may think of recent decades as the age of experts when ordinary folk do not repair their own automobiles nor build their own houses so they naturally leave schooling to the profession. In addition, changing family patterns and economic conditions result in more single-parent families and more women at work outside of home. Most small communities have increasing numbers of senior citizens so that it is not uncommon for only one-third of the taxpayers to have children in school. Some conditions may make parental participation in schooling more difficult but there is increasing disenchantment with the experts. From many directions we are being urged to build learning upon the natural relationship between parent and child. Moreover, some issues such as those related to the environment, AIDS, human rights, employment and the need for lifelong learning pull school and community together much more than did traditional topics in literature, history, science and mathematics. It may be more difficult than it once was but, in our view, there are compelling reasons to increase and improve the involvement of parents and community in schooling. The most important incentive, of course, is that student learning improves.

## Closer to Home

If "smallness" is related to involvement there should be plenty of it in a state such as Nebraska, which has 600 school systems of fewer than 100 students. In the combined states of Colorado, Kansas, Missouri, Nebraska, North Dakota, South Dakota and Wyoming, of 2 055 school systems, 83 percent have fewer than 1 000 students.

If legislation can bring about involvement it should prevail in the province of Saskatchewan where each school has an elected local board that acts in an advisory capacity to the system board. The result is a typical rural jurisdiction with more than 50 elected board members, about 75 teachers and only the superintendent (director) in an administrative role without teaching responsibilities. This ratio of leaders to elected board members at 50 to 1 is far different from an urban system and causes many difficulties related to role clarity. The same is true in Alberta where the school Act provides for school councils. Many school systems include parents and community in system evaluations, reviews and planning studies. We draw upon our experience in such projects to share some views of parents and community.

**Views of Program**. The provision of program in small schools is a major challenge particularly in periods of economic hardship, declining enrolments and increasing expectations. It is important to know the views of  parents and community as a major consideration in planning and in decision making.

Table 5.1 shows the responses of parents to program options in the Big Valley School Division. The format of the table is a way to focus attention on current programs but also to provide an orientation toward the future.

**Table 5.1**
**Parents' Views of School Program in Terms of**
**Recommended Emphasis in the Future (N = 557)**

| Program | Percentage | | |
|---|---|---|---|
| | Less | Same | More |
| 1. Basic skills | 0.4 | 43.5 | 56.1[1] |
| 2. For slow learners | 2.2 | 37.9 | 59.9 |
| 3. For the gifted | 15.3 | 61.9 | 22.8 |
| 4. Music–regular | 13.9 | 63.7 | 22.4 |
| 5. Music–band | 28.9 | 53.8 | 17.2 |
| 6. Fine Arts | 10.2 | 70.2 | 19.6 |
| 7. Core French | 36.7 | 45.8 | 17.5 |
| 8. French Immersion | 61.3 | 27.9 | 10.9 |
| 9. Other languages | 46.2 | 35.4 | 18.4 |
| 10. Counselling–career | 4.1 | 34.0 | 61.9 |
| 11. Counselling–personal | 3.1 | 36.0 | 60.9 |
| 12. Native studies | 35.3 | 56.1 | 8.7 |
| 13. Work experience | 12.1 | 52.6 | 35.2 |
| 14. Life skills | 3.0 | 35.1 | 61.9 |
| 15. New programs | 12.7 | 61.1 | 26.2 |
| 16. Alternate programs | 3.2 | 48.2 | 48.6 |
| 17. Computer related | 1.9 | 34.9 | 63.2 |

[1] Percentages may not total 100 because of rounding off and blank responses.

Program features, of course, vary from place to place but they can include areas of controversy such as the teaching of French in western Canada. The results are typical of rural jurisdictions within which we have worked including a majority call for increased emphasis on basic skills, programs for students with special needs, counselling, life skills (including drug, alcohol and sex education) and computer related features. Many parents will add notes of caution about programs for the future such as, "All this must take into consideration the available funding and the limits placed upon it by small enrolment" and "I am very concerned about the workload our students carry—I feel we must be very careful how we expand."

**Views of School and System Operations**. Again it is relatively easy to determine parents' perceptions of how the school and system are run day-by-day. In Table 5.2 we show results that we have found to be representative of parents in small school-communities. Generally about two-thirds have positive feelings about teachers, a large majority feel welcome at the school and fewer than half believe they have a voice in school matters. Reactions to discipline, principals and superintendents, of course, vary greatly among school-communities even within the same school system. Choice of courses for students is an aspect about which there is a mixed reaction.

Many rural or remote school systems in western Canada have from 8 to 12 schools and we usually find parents' views of the school much more positive than they are of the school system. The table shows this very clearly. The lowest percentages of positive responses in this case, as in others in our experience, are related to the lack of effective involvement of parents and the lack of communication about what the board and super-intendent are doing and how they do it. This point is reinforced by examining Table 5.3 containing information from a rural Alberta system more than 1 000 kilometers from Big Valley.

The point we wish to emphasize is that parents and community have strong views about various aspects of schooling and share them willingly if given an opportunity. Many comments reflect deep-seated concerns:

## Table 5.2
## Parents' Views of School and System Operations (N = 537)

## Percentages of positive responses in a rural Saskatchewan system

|  | School Operations (20 items) | System Operations (16 items) |
|---|---|---|
| Over 80% | School is kept clean, support staff friendly, a good school, I feel welcome at school | |
| 70-79% | Homework, attendance, standards, reporting, student-teacher relations, students enjoy school | Buildings are kept in good repair |
| 60-69% | Values at home and school, home-school communication, teachers, the principal, library, class size, teachers give extra help, discipline | Provision of an adequate educational program Principals |
| 50-59% | | Support staff, teachers |
| 40-49% | Choice of courses Voice in school matters | |
| 30-39% | | Policy implementation, administrators listening to parents, leadership and direction, long-range planning |
| Under 30% | | Board members open to new ideas, governance, fiscal management, board response to parents, fair treatment of school, public voice, two-way communication with parents |

**Table 5.3**
**Parents' Views of School System Factors (N = 264)**
**Level of Satisfaction in a County System in Alberta**

**Top 10 of 71 items (in descending order)**

Accessibility of teachers to parents
Bus drivers
Recognition of accomplishments of students
School buildings up-to-date
Diploma (provincial) exam results
Buildings—maintenance and repair
Support staff in schools
Core curriculum programs
Buildings—safety and grounds
Caretakers—care of school

**Lowest 10 of 71 items (in descending order)**

County administrator's responsiveness to community concerns
Guidance and counselling services
The Board's annual report
School closure policy
Board relations with the community
Board representation of ratepayers' concerns
Level of provincial financial support
Board responsiveness to community concerns
Board's decisions in view of financial demands
Opportunity to influence the County education budget

*I wish there wasn't so much animosity among community people regarding sending children to another school.*

*Numbers are a statisticians game. The quality of education depends more on the attitude, motivation, enthusiasm, support and creativity of teachers, administrators and community.*

*Parents have little control over the education of their children.*

❖   ❖   ❖

Clearly the views of parents and community reported here provide "serious stuff" for reflection, discussion and action. Let's now turn our attention to examples of action.

## Turning to Illustrations

There are exciting developments in schools in sparsely populated areas. In these cases leaders are moving beyond comparing small schools to large schools and are beginning to capitalize on the potential advantages of their context. Parents and teachers, schools and communities, are coming together for the benefit of learners of all ages. We present four examples in order to help leaders think more about their ideas for further developments in their school-community.

On North Haven Island, off the coast of Maine, the 400 residents and 8 teachers of the K-12 school have developed and implemented an exemplary vocational education program for the 84 students in the school. The program is sensitive to both the advantages and limitations of living on an island. Emphasis is on the whole, integrated school-community. Instruction includes role playing, "hands on" learning, resource persons and field trips to the mainland for urban experiences. Special attention is given to how students perceive isolation and to establishing the view that it is "okay" to stay on the island—that you don't need to leave to succeed.

The Mid-continent Regional Educational Laboratory (McREL) has a Rural Schools and Development Project. Included is Belle Fourche, South Dakota, a community of 5 000 where a special effort is being made to integrate the school with the community so that the curriculum is more meaningful, cognitively complex, integrated and contextual—a school without walls. Two outcomes are students being responsible for a twice-a-week radio show on the local commercial station which is part of a corporation created by the students called THIS, Limited. The radio show is called HEAR THIS; the refreshment stand is EAT THIS; a T-shirt printing business is known as WEAR THIS; and the dinner-theatre is WATCH THIS.

The San Luis Valley in southern Colorado has a rich history but serious, current problems related to high unemployment, poverty, low achievement, high drop-out rates, teacher morale and accusations of prejudice against the predominantly Hispanic population. A regional education agency, McREL and IBM are working with local community and school leaders to redesign schools, revitalize the curriculum and change boundaries if necessary. Included as well is intensive staff development focused on "Power Teaching," higher order thinking skills, whole language, motivation and student evaluation. Adams State College is revising teacher training programs accordingly. Community leaders are receiving assistance in community development strategies so that the schools and community may develop together.

The Frontier School Division in northern Manitoba has established parental involvement as a high priority. A *Parental Involvement Handbook* (actually a large binder) has been prepared to guide efforts at the school-community level. As one parent pointed out many adults had attended residential schools where there was absolutely no parental involvement—the school determined food, medicine, hair cuts and curriculum. Now he reports ". . . grandparents coming to *our* school who never would have thought that they could walk with ease through the halls of the school and be welcomed, be able to sit in the staffroom with teachers and have tea . . . that's a long way, really a long way."

## Relating

Thinking is an individual effort compared to relating to others in order that our thoughts may be extended by language and by dialogue. We need to be reminded as well that dialogue includes suspending our assumptions about "what is" and "what might be done." It also means concentrating on trends and issues more than on events. The following questions may assist in relating with others about the voices of parents and community.

1. What are the "big-picture" factors affecting parental and community involvement in your school system? Some considerations could include history, changes in the family structure and values, population shifts, economic conditions, and community patterns in religious, cultural and recreational activities. What are the risks and opportunities for better integration of school and community?

2. What are the views of adults about schooling at the present time? Are there recent surveys? What would parents and community members list as five strengths and five weaknesses of the school system?

3. How can we integrate more parental involvement and a more community-based curriculum with what is known about needs of students and with recent developments in education?

4. Are all available leadership resources being utilized in integrating school-community development?

5. Some claim that teachers and administrators are reluctant to promote meaningful parental and community involvement in schooling—they wish to be left alone. Do you find this to be the case? If so, what can be done?

6. What information do I have to support the idea that increased parental and community involvement is of benefit to students, to teachers, to administrators, to parents, to the community and to me?

7. What meaning does the heading of this chapter have to me in my context—"They want you to come but they don't listen?"

8. How can I make parental and community involvement better in my school system?

## Planning

The idea in this section is to get beyond words and to take some action in order to further parental and community involvement in schools. The guidelines suggested are based upon what has been learned about the reality of schooling in sparsely populated areas, about change processes in school systems and about visionary leadership. An attempt has been made to outline appropriate plans for leaders who are just beginning to give parent-community involvement attention and for those who are at a stage of redesign.

## Initiating

First steps would be personal, low profile activities in order to get more information about the topic. As noted earlier in this chapter, much is being written and said about closer links between schools and communities. Among other things it is important to consider levels of involvement from signing report cards, attending school events, coming to interviews, attending meetings, assisting in developing programs such as outdoor education or community development, to acting as a resource person or volunteer. These considerations are important in order to clarify expectations and to begin to imagine what could be better—a vision. The expected outcome at this stage is a personal position including an articulated vision and a commitment of the time and energy you as leader will devote to attaining that vision.

If your personal position is formulated, it is time to share your vision and to state your position perhaps at a principals' meeting, a board meeting or a parent meeting. The vision becomes not only articulated but shared in some form. Follow-up activities could include:

1. Preparation of a community profile including age groups, population trends, cultural-ethnic background, sources of income, use of recreational facilities, church membership, business trends and so forth.

2. A survey of public views of schooling by means of questionnaires, random telephone interviews, face-to-face interviews, formulation of an advisory group, etc. The survey could also reveal current levels of involvement in schooling.

The results should indicate what gaps there are between the vision and reality. The challenge then is to formulate an action (implementation) plan to close the gaps. Any action will represent a change. Planning for change includes listing factors which will either support your efforts or present barriers. Our experience suggests that in many school-communities the following factors would "enter the picture" if efforts were made to increase the involvement of parents-community:

1. Supporting—benefits to students, smallness (less "red tape"), community resources and needs, public interest.

2. Hindering—history of little involvement, tendency of administrators not to listen, reluctance of teachers, lack of clarity regarding public and professional roles, teacher workload and lack of goal clarity.

3. Overriding all of these factors is quality and continuity of leadership including vision and the skills necessary to orchestrate all of the many factors which affect change processes.

Experience in school systems such as Frontier and New Haven suggests that professional staff have to approach the community with respect for local people, traditions and values. People in those jurisdictions have also found that efforts have to be focused upon particular problems or projects ranging all the way from improving attendance to launching a new career-awareness program. Without goal clarity and monitoring, early success cannot be fully realized and initiatives tend to lose momentum. Projects are like a diet—they are easier to start than they are to continue.

## Redesigning

The wording "continuing" has not been used as a heading because it implies continuing "as is" and it is, therefore, not in keeping with the spirit of this book. Redesigning, on the other hand, means making adjustments along the way in the light of results and changing circumstances in order to better accomplish what was intended.

Redesign requires systematic monitoring (feedback) so that there is a basis for redesign, yet this aspect of change processes is often neglected. It is necessary to know to what extent intended results are being realized. It may be as simple as knowing whether or not average attendance has improved, if more parents are listening to students read at home or if there is more community participation in career days. More comprehensive monitoring could compare current survey results with those two years ago. Efforts become meaningful when results are communicated and linked to vision.

Redesign also includes discussion of outcomes to date with various stakeholders, analysis of environmental factors and formulation of plans for the next time period. Support is required in terms of continuing interest, leadership, integration of school-level and system-level initiatives, time, money and organizational structures, such as work groups and communication channels, to keep up the interest and participation. There also must be pressure in relation to clear expectations and monitoring. There must be a ready answer if someone asks "Who cares about the involvement of parents and community in schooling?"

If leadership has been shared and if processes of school-community interaction have been effective, representatives of all stakeholders will care deeply about the involvement of parents and community in schooling. It will be seen as central, not as something that is fine if you can manage it. If certain advocates left the school or community, expectations and processes would remain—leadership for involvement of the parents and community in schooling would have been built into the organization.

It is time now to write down in a calendar or journal, on not more than one page, what our personal plan is to promote further or redesigned involvement of parents and community in schools. The intention is that this be a specific action plan for the near future—within a week. Later more collaborative, strategic planning would be done. For now consider asking parent advisory committees for their views, checking the local newspaper for items about schooling or having lunch with a community leader.

## Thinking Again

The thinking at the beginning of this chapter, relating to others and planning/doing/observing/reading have left us now with new thoughts about parent and community involvement in schooling. Repeated cycles of thinking, relating and planning will provide us with continued learning in this vital aspect of schooling and with preparation in a key component of strategic planning—providing for and listening to the voices of parents and community.

*Teachers should change their attitude toward parents.*

- a parent

# References

Frontier School Division #48 (1984). *Parental involvement handbook.* Winnipeg, Manitoba, 1402 Notre Dame Avenue, R3E 3G5: Frontier S.D. #48.

Gjelton, T. (1978). *Schooling in isolated communities.* Portland, Maine 04112, Box 13: North Haven Project for Career Development.

Knudson, B. (1990). *A study of the principals' role in planning for increased parental involvement.* Unpublished M.Ed. project, College of Education, University of Saskatchewan, Saskatoon, Saskatchewan, S7N 0W0.

Mid-continent Regional Educational Laboratory (1989). *What's noteworthy on rural schools and community development?* Aurora: Colorado, 12500 E. Iliff Avenue, Suite 201, 80014.

Saskatchewan Educational Leadership Unit (1988). *Direction for the 1990's (A planning study of a rural school division).* College of Education, University of Saskatchewan, Saskatoon, Saskatchewan, S7N 0W0.

—(1990). *Planning for the 1990's (A study for a rural school division).* College of Education, University of Saskatchewan, Saskatoon, Saskatchewan, S7N 0W0.

Schmuck, P.A. & Schmuck, R.A. (1990). *Democratic participation in small-town schools.* Eugene, Oregon: University of Oregon.

# 6

# Voices of Teachers and Principals

*It all depends on the teacher.*
- a parent referring to multigrade classrooms

How do teachers make news in the 1990s? We have heard recently, through the media, of a grade 2 teacher who was introducing her students to environmental issues and had one of her students selected to go to the United Nations "Earth Day." Last evening's news included a story of teachers and students from an Alberta school who are packaging food for the food bank. Teachers who lead choirs, coach teams and organize field trips certainly impress the public. Eliot Wigginton's *Foxfire* program has won international acclaim. There are also headlines about teacher shortages, cases of sexual misconduct, the promotion of hatred and the rights of teachers with aids. Public attention is one thing but even more central to our purposes are the comments about teachers when students arrive home from school and teachers' views of schooling in sparsely populated areas. Attention has been given in preceding chapters to the views that students and the public have of teachers. It is time now to consider teachers' views in more detail.

Planning studies, system evaluations, observations and informal discussions with hundreds of rural teachers form the data base for this chapter. For the sake of continuity and interpretive validity responses of teachers in the Big Valley School Division to a questionnaire will be shared in some detail. As well, comments from selected Alberta Studies will be included. In the planning and redesigning sections recent practice and developments will be reported.

# Thinking

*The Big Picture*

Our first challenge is to think of teaching in relation to changing environmental "big picture" factors. The other day we heard someone wonder "what history" teachers in east European countries are teaching. We did learn this past summer that countries in the European Community co-operated to launch a satellite in 1989 for educational broadcasting. Some have doubted the motives of governmental and educational leaders in both Europe and North America saying that we are urging teachers to talk more, to work together in teams—to make education more public—at the very time when governments want to watch education more closely. It is common now to hear political leaders speak of human capital and the importance of schooling in preparing a country for the international market place. These factors plus societal concerns about the environment, substance abuse, AIDS, employment, poverty and peace all filter down to and weigh upon the classroom teacher. More specifically, for example, immigration policies result in teachers having increasing numbers of students for whom English is not the first language, sexual misconduct cases have led teacher organizations to warn their members "not to get too close," enrolment decline raises the possibility of redundancy, the continuing knowledge explosion threatens everyone with being uninformed, and most innovations related to an integrated curriculum challenge teachers to "tie it all together" and to help all students, even those with special needs, to do so. To top it off, increasing numbers of parents in the work force make it more difficult for parents and teachers to meet, let alone work together, increasing demands from the public have left principals with less time for working with teachers and budget problems have usually resulted in reduced centra l office support for teachers. Fortunately, most teachers in sparsely populated areas do not have as much violence in schools as urban teachers do. The impact of the "big picture" in making teaching more demanding and more complex is dramatic.

Parallelling the increasing challenge for teachers from external factors are some supporting developments. Teacher qualifications have increased greatly, most teacher education programs have improved, salaries relative to most other professions are better and teacher professional organizations in most parts of the world have become prominent in shaping education. Learning resource centres are central to most schools, distance education offers new possibilities and government curriculum materials typically are prepared with more attention to the needs of teachers. It is increasingly recognized that the professional development of teachers is an ongoing endeavor and more and more opportunities are provided for teachers.

Rural contexts, of course, vary greatly, but generally entail both advantages and disadvantages for teachers. Lower pupil-teacher ratios are offset by more time required in planning instruction for multigrade classrooms. Advantages in lifestyle are countered by isolation. "Smallness" makes change faster at times but more vulnerable to personnel factors and "local politics." Reactions from teachers as well as from formal studies reveal that whether teaching in a sparsely populated area is a plus or a minus all depends upon how the teacher views the situation—some see it as "second best and second rate" because they could not get a job in "the city" whereas some see it as an opportunity to make schooling particularly rewarding for students.

### Closer to Home

The general picture, of course, may not apply to a particular situation so information from the local scene is crucial. Even within a jurisdiction each student, parent, teacher, administrator, board member and community stakeholder will see a school, school program or teacher differently. This is the complication of "multiple realities" and it is part of the complexity with which leaders must grapple. We mention this point here because in interviewing every teacher in a school their responses were so varied we often wondered if they were talking about the same place or the same principal. For emphasis, we share below the following teacher comments about their principal in a K-12 school of 345 students and 19 teachers.

*"He lets you go ahead and do whatever."*
*"He does what the division wants him to do—he himself is not innovative."*
*"Not always supportive. Sees it as a 9–12 school."*
*"Seldom go for help because we get a smart answer."*
*"No pats so leaves you wondering if you're appreciated."*

Five Primary Teachers

*"Fails to communicate and keep staff informed."*
*"Support is there."*
*"Personally no complaints."*
*"Support? Damn little —he did not even know what reading pro-*

*gram we went into."*
*"If I tell him I have a problem, it's perceived as a weakness."*
*"Pops in—shows he's interested and finds out what you're*
*doing."*

Six Middle Grade Teachers

*"I'm really lucky Mr. X is such good support."*
*"He sets program, knows his teachers and what they are good at."*
*"Lots of heartaches—principals want their jobs to run smoothly*
*so they must keep community and kids happy so they don't*
*worry too much about staff."*
*"Reasonably good."*
*"He is supportive of ideas and suggestions made by teachers."*

Five High School Teachers

*no comment!*

Vice-principal

*"We weren't always a K-12 school—the Board decided. Elemen-*
*tary teachers are somewhat threatened by high school stu-*
*dents. . . . We tend to have staff around for a long time. . . . they*
*get set in their ways."*

Principal

So how well would you say the principal is doing? Clearly it depends upon which teachers you ask, let alone the voices of students and parents-community.

Despite multiple realities it is useful to consider the general picture as a starting point for discussion and clarification. We shall share some data from the Big Valley School Division teachers in order to promote thought and reflection on the readers' own context.

**Teachers' Views of Program.** As with parents, teachers were asked to consider program features with respect to the emphasis they thought each should receive in the future. Results are summarized in Table 6.1. The percentage of parents recommending more emphasis in each aspect of the program is also noted so that teacher and parent perceptions may be compared. The areas of greatest agreement include more emphasis on counselling, life skills and basic skills. It is interesting to note that more teachers believe the gifted, fine arts (including regular music), personal counselling and work experience should receive increased attention whereas more parents support strengthened programs for slow learners, computers and other innovations. Teachers and parents generally agree that language and cultural programs are receiving enough attention. In Big Valley most students support additions to counselling programs. The writers wish to emphasize that students, parents and teachers have many views of how programs should be altered in the future. Areas of agreement and disagreement raise points for clarification, discussion and action. Underlying varying perceptions is the question of "to whom do schools belong?" Who should make program decisions and how should they be made? This kind of internal analysis is central to the strategic planning process.

### Table 6.1 Teachers' Views of School Program in Terms of Recommended Emphasis in the Future (N = 82)

| Program | | Less | Same | More | Percentage (More - parents) |
|---|---|---|---|---|---|
| 1. | Basic skills | 0.0 | 40.7 | 59.3[1] | 56.1 |
| 2. | For slow learners | 1.2 | 42.7 | 43.9 | 59.9[2] |
| 3. | For the gifted | 7.3 | 57.3 | 35.4 | 22.8 |
| 4. | Music–regular | 8.5 | 47.6 | 43.9 | 22.4 |
| 5. | Music–band | 17.6 | 63.5 | 18.9 | 17.2 |
| 6. | Fine Arts | 7.4 | 54.3 | 38.3 | 19.6 |
| 7. | Core French | 43.8 | 45.0 | 11.3 | 17.5 |
| 8. | French Immersion | 59.2 | 34.2 | 6.6 | 10.9 |
| 9. | Other languages | 41.9 | 45.9 | 12.2 | 18.4 |
| 10. | Counselling–career | 2.7 | 28.0 | 69.3 | 61.9 |
| 11. | Counselling– personal | 1.3 | 24.7 | 74.0 | 60.9 |
| 12. | Native studies | 26.4 | 62.5 | 11.1 | 8.7 |
| 13. | Work experience | 2.8 | 51.4 | 45.8 | 35.2 |
| 14. | Life skills | 1.2 | 35.8 | 63.0 | 61.9 |
| 15. | New programs | 31.3 | 57.5 | 11.3 | 26.2 |
| 16. | Alternate programs | 9.1 | 45.5 | 45.5 | 48.6 |
| 17. | Computer related | 3.7 | 60.5 | 35.8 | 63.2 |

[1] Percentages will not always total 100 because of rounding off and blank responses.
[2] Differences of 10 or more percentage points between teacher and parent views have been noted with an arrow. The arrow points in the direction of the higher percentage.

**Teachers' Views of the School as a Workplace.** There is increasing emphasis upon the need for teachers to engage in continuing professional development. At the same time as there is long-standing concern about a decline in teacher competency after about 6 years of experience. Table 6.2, which follows, reports the Big Valley teachers' perceptions of their workplace, and Table 6.3 shows their reaction to professional development. It is interesting to notice that over 80 percent of the teachers are pleased with their teaching assignment and think teachers and students get along well,  yet only about 50 percent sense a "togetherness" among staff and feel that morale is high (see Table 6.2). This result, together with other work we have done, leads us to state that student-teacher relations are typically better than staff relations regardless of the size of the school. Related to this are the mixed reactions of teachers to school-based professional development (see Table 6.3) and yet two-thirds of teachers would like more. All of this points to the need for more leadership so that there is integration of professional development at the individual, school and system levels.

**Views of the School Division.** On average, 62 percent of the teachers have positive views of their workplace (school) whereas only 52 percent have positive views of the School Division. More details are provided in Table 6.4. It can be seen that the most agreement is in relation to school building maintenance, the range of programs offered, provision of instructional resources, hiring good teachers (We like us!) and the Board and Superintendent being open to new ideas. Approximately one quarter of the teachers have negative feelings about fair treatment of schools, two-way communication with teachers, hiring of adequate support staff, responding to concerns of teachers, doing long-range planning and giving leadership and direction. For many items large numbers of teacher responses were neutral, reflecting, in all likelihood, lack of information and communication. Compare Table 6.4 to Table 6.5 drawn from a rural system in Alberta. Note again that strengths are seen in relation to program, staff and student achievement. Other than concern about guidance and counselling lowest levels of satisfaction centre around involvement in decision-making, finance, and Board-community communication.

The extent to which any items should be acted upon depends upon our vision of an effective school system. We expect that the pictures presented in this chapter are something less than our vision, just as they were for the leaders of the Big Valley School Division and the Alberta County System.

### Table 6.2 Teachers' Views of Their Workplace —Selected Items (N = 82)

| Item | Percentage | | |
|---|---|---|---|
| | Positive | Neutral | Negative |
| 1. The pupil-teacher ratios are appropriate | 55.1 | 6.3 | 38.8[1] |
| 2. Teachers have adequate preparation time | 21.0 | 8.6 | 70.4 |
| 3. I find my workload acceptable | 54.3 | 14.8 | 30.8 |
| 4. In general, I teach in areas for which I am trained | 63.5 | 11.4 | 15.2 |
| 5. I am generally pleased with my teaching experience | 88.5 | 7.4 | 6.2 |
| 6. There is a "togetherness" within the staff | 54.3 | 4.9 | 40.7 |
| 7. Decision-making is democratic | 66.6 | 16.7 | 16.7 |
| 8. Problems are solved—not just ignored | 53.1 | 13.6 | 33.3 |
| 9. Teachers' opinions are valued | 77.7 | 8.6 | 13.6 |
| 10. Any staff member may assume leadership responsibilities | 71.3 | 17.5 | 11.3 |
| 11. Teachers enjoy informal "get-togethers" | 66.6 | 13.6 | 19.7 |
| 12. The morale of teachers is high | 54.6 | 18.2 | 27.3 |
| 13. Teachers offer extra help to students | 86.6 | 12.2 | 1.2 |
| 14. Students and teachers get along well | 84.1 | 8.5 | 7.3 |
| 15. There is good communication in the school | 60.5 | 12.3 | 27.2 |
| 16. This school is a good place to work | 75.7 | 15.4 | 9.0 |
| 17. I get appreciation/recognition | 52.5 | 22.5 | 25.1 |
| 18. I have adequate influence | 60.0 | 18.8 | 21.3 |
| 19. This School Division is a good place to work | 81.7 | 12.2 | 6.1 |
| 20. The students like school | 71.6 | 19.8 | 8.6 |

[1] Percentages may not total 100 due to rounding off and blank responses.

## Table 6.3 Teachers' Views of Professional Development

| | Item | Percentage Positive | Neutral | Negative |
|---|---|---|---|---|
| 1. | There are opportunities for PD | 86.4 | 9.9 | 3.7 |
| 2. | I am satisfied with division-wide PD | 63.0 | 13.6 | 23.4 |
| 3. | PD programs are available re: up-to-date teaching methods | 65.6 | 14.6 | 9.8 |
| 4. | PD programs are available for program development/implementation | 66.3 | 18.8 | 15.1 |
| 5. | There are PD activities on program evaluation | 34.1 | 26.6 | 39.3 |
| 6. | Our school has organized PD activities | 57.5 | 18.8 | 23.8 |
| 7. | Teachers have adequate input into planning PD programs | 54.9 | 23.2 | 21.9 |
| 8. | Generally, PD activities meet my needs | 49.4 | 21.0 | 29.6 |
| 9. | I would like to see more school-based PD | 68.7 | 26.2 | 5.0 |

## Table 6.4 Teachers' Views of School System Operations (N = 82)
### Percentage of positive responses in a rural Saskatchewan System

| | |
|---|---|
| Over 80% | Maintenance of buildings |
| 70-79% | Providing a wide range of programs for students |
| 69-69% | Supplying instructional resources<br>Hiring good teachers<br>Being open to new ideas |
| 50-59% | Governance<br>Providing for policy reviews<br>Appointing good principals<br>Providing adequate support staff<br>Leadership and direction |
| 40-49% | Giving the public a say in running schools<br>Responding to concerns of teachers |
| 30-39% | Long-range  planning<br>Maintaining two-way communication<br>Community relations<br>Fiscal management |
| Under 30% | Treating schools fairly |

**Table 6.5 Employees' Views of School System Factors N = 60 (including 30 teachers, 8 administrators, 12 support staff—school level) Level of Satisfaction in a County System in Alberta**

**Top 10 of 71 items (in descending order)**
> Instructional programs
> Diploma (provincial) exam results
> Accessibility of teachers to parents
> Instructional staff in schools
> Achievement test results
> Recognition of accomplishments of students
> Bus drivers
> Support staff in schools
> Staff—behaviour and attitude
> Buses—safety and maintenance

**Lowest of 71 items (in descending order)**
> Board represents ratepayers' concerns
> The Boards' Annual Report
> Board relations with the community
> School closure policy
> Board responsiveness to community concerns
> Guidance and counselling services
> Level of local taxation for education
> Boards' decisions in view of financial demands
> Level of provincial financial support
> Opportunity to influence the County education budget

**Principals.** As for teachers, powerful external and local factors are making the world of the school principal in sparsely populated areas much more complex. An Ontario survey reported most principals feeling less effective than they were five years ago. That decline is related to the title of *What's Worth Fighting for in the Principalship?* by Michael Fullan, 1988. How do principals in your system feel about their effectiveness?

Studies of the principal indicate that they have various responsibilities related to students, staff, parents, curriculum, instruction, budget, physical facility and so on. Indications are that they devote most of their time to management tasks—crisis management—although they would like to be more involved in instructional leadership. Hall, Hord and associates (1984), after studying principals' behaviour as change agents, categorized principals as *managers* who "help things happen," *initiators* who "make things happen" or *responders* who "let things happen." We should avoid labelling people but it is important to recognize that principals, like teachers or superintendents, have different priorities and different styles. From our experience and as pointed out in the literature there is a general picture of a principal as a person who hustles about having dozens of short interactions each day in an attempt "to keep the lid on."

The rural context, as for teachers, typically has both advantages and disadvantages for principals. Major advantages are the potential for knowing everyone well—from pupils to the public—and thus being in a position to personalize the school. The problem is that most principals in small schools have to teach most of the day. There is time only to look after administrative details and crises. Anything beyond a responder or manager role requires extra effort on personal time.

While we do believe that a keen principal can make a difference faster in a rural than in an urban context, our experience supports those who think that we have exaggerated the difference a principal can make. The approach which we support is depicted in Figure 6.5 (see following page). In this model a principal's instructional leadership is seen to depend upon factors such as the community, the school system and personal attributes. Do you agree that these considerations do make a difference to what principals can do? In turn the principal in a large school affects students indirectly through having an impact on school climate and organization. We have found that in small schools principals directly affect students when they have classroom responsibilities. The model depicted was used by Hallinger and associates in a school improvement study of 98 elementary schools in Tennessee. Their findings underline the importance of mission (vision), focus on student learning and high teacher expectations. As well they emphasize the impact of community and organizational variables on the principal.

Principals in the Big Valley School Division were greatly influenced by community and organizational factors. In one case the families, community and school were co-operating to establish a small park by the school and yet dissension was caused by a man who was chair of the local board of trustees and also caretaker of the school. In another school, the principal had followed a long-time, highly-respected principal who had retired but whose wife was still on staff. In a third situation the principal, his wife and three children had to live in a trailer because the local board insisted that the principal live in the community. Two of the principals made the following comments:

Figure 6.1 A Framework for Considering
Principals as Instructional Leaders

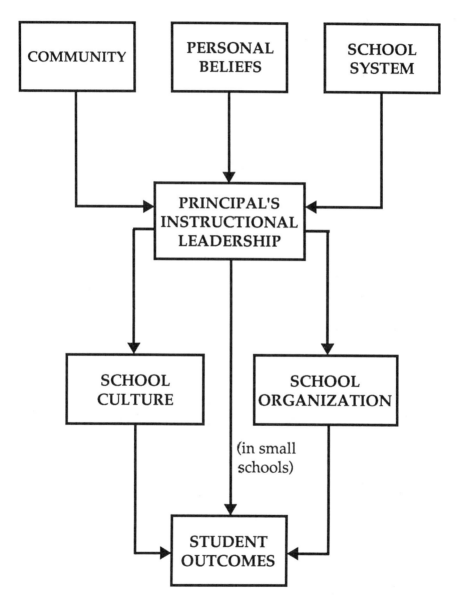

Hallinger and Associates, 1991

❖  ❖  ❖

*In a school like this (five teachers, K-12) it is possible to teach in-
stead of herd students. I, as a principal, have no free time so do
'management by walking around.' The changes to small Saskatchewan schools will only add fuel to a fire that is already creating
suicide conditions on the farm.*

*Children should not be sacrificed to keep the town alive a few
more years . . . one person is one-quarter of the entire staff so a
negative thinker or someone who is less responsible has a greater
significance than might otherwise be felt.*

❖  ❖  ❖

## Turning to Illustrations

There are many examples of happenings related to teaching. The general
belief seems to be that the world of the teacher is not likely to get any
simpler so the challenge is to meet the increased pressures with additional
support, recognition and understanding. Four examples illustrate these
developments.

An Induction for the Beginning Teacher program, sponsored by
the College of Education at California State University, Chico,
operates in five remote northern counties of the state. Dr. Victoria
Bernhardt, Director of IBT, recently hosted the third annual "Cele-
bration of Success" for 90 new and experienced teachers.

The IBT includes 55 hours of seminars and 60 hours of field work
for which five units of credit are given. In addition to this commitment the beginning teachers must locate their own learning partners by asking experienced teachers if they will participate. These
peer coaches receive six credit units for 62 hours of instruction
which includes preparation for peer coaching. About 60 additional
hours are devoted to observing and assisting the beginning teachers. According to reports all participants enjoy the success that
comes with commitment to teaching.

In Ontario a colloquium has been established by the Faculty of Education, University of Toronto, and five school jurisdictions in order to integrate preservice and inservice education and to work towards improved change processes in schools. School systems must apply to be involved and are chosen for a three to five year period depending upon their commitment to the ongoing professional development of teachers and to school improvement. Faculty of education students, teachers in the field, administrators and faculty collaborate on a regular basis in relation to their mutual goal of learning more about learning and teaching.

re cognition!

In order to promote awareness of teaching excellence in the province, the Government of Alberta in 1989 began an *Excellence in Teaching Awards Program*. With the support and involvement of education partners 255 local awards were presented in 1990 and 20 of these were chosen to also receive a provincial award. Nominations must be endorsed by the principal, the superintendent, a teaching colleague and two members from the public. Nominations are then reviewed by a committee which is made up of representatives of all stakeholder groups. According to the Minister of Education the program "... serves as a reminder to every one that teachers deserve praise and appreciation for their commitment to the hard work of helping our children learn and grow" - Press release, September 5, 1990.

> The Saskatchewan Teachers' Federation recently completed a Study of Teaching. Over 1 000 teachers from across the province responded to a request to describe both successful and unsuccessful teaching experience. Analysis of the behaviours associated with each revealed that success is related to creating opportunities for students to learn, leading students to learn and classroom management. Lack of success is related to minimal effort, disrespect for students, poor decisions and ineffective performance of teaching skills. Analysts concluded that lack of success "really hurts a teacher" and they tend to persist in trying to turn such events around. The STF General Secretary claims that the study offers a new vision for teacher education, for individual teachers and for the profession.

## Relating

Survey data and our experiences make it clear that the relationships among teachers, board members and superintendents in rural contexts tend to be problematic, yet there are shining examples of systems with voices being heard, shared vision and vitality. A common feeling among teachers is that when the superintendent appears there must be a problem and that elected board members are beginning to interfere in professional matters. Clarification of roles and a sense of everyone pulling together likely begins by relating informally with teachers on the street corner or in the staffroom. You may wish to gain insight into some of the questions listed. *not just when problems*

1. What do teachers care about from day to day? What aspects of their work are they excited about? What are their concerns?

2. What indicators demonstrate teacher "connectedness" among instructional changes, new curriculum, professional development, supervision, evaluation and emphasis on student outcomes?

3. What are the indicators of high levels of teacher interaction within a school related to school and system development?

4. How do teachers view the board, the central office staff and their involvement in system decision-making processes?

5. How comfortable are teachers, particularly new ones, with community expectations and community support?

6. How is the system helping teachers to feel that their work is recognized and appreciated?

7. What are the principals' views of their role, the system pressures and support and community?

As a leader how well informed do you feel about the beliefs and priorities of the professional staff? You may wish to formalize or strengthen relationships by considering scheduled school visits, membership on committees and more prominent staff leadership in strategic planning processes.

## Planning

On the basis of your thoughts, your position and what you have learned by relating to staff you may wish to take some action at the system level. Our experience shows that leading school systems in sparsely populated areas have carefully considered the impact of the local context on teachers/principals and have policy related to the following topics:

1. Teacher recruitment and orientation programs,

2. Incentives for teachers in terms of housing, professional development programs and study leaves,

3. Flexible personnel policies to permit various term appointments including system leadership roles,

4. Promotion of a caring climate when staff members have health or personal problems,

5. Emphasis on a flatter organization with improved channels for communication and clarity regarding various public and professional roles,

6. The heavy responsibility of school system leaders to establish direction, set priorities, clarify expectations and balance pressure with support, and

7. The importance of having personnel practices and policies consistent with current issues and developments such as gender equity, human rights and opportunities for minority groups.

The points above address some of the problems and possibilities related to teachers and principals in small school-communities. It is abundantly clear that there is much more to leadership than simply leaving teachers alone.

## Thinking Again

Our conviction is that we must begin to give the staffing of small schools much more attention in the light of both contextual and organizational changes. An increasing percentage of beginning teachers do not want to go into remote areas and many who do are frustrated at the loss of privacy and limited social life in most small communities. What incentives do you think could be offered to attract and retain the services of teachers and principals? Would it help to be able, in all honesty, to invite them to join an exciting school system with a sense of direction, a feeling of accomplishment, cutting edge personnel policies and strategic planning processes which effectively involve all stakeholders?

> *Yes, our principal is the most decent guy you have ever met. He is kind, considerate and caring. He is also so happy and understanding. He has real sense for kids. I wish more principals were like this fine man.*
>
> - a student

### References

Alberta Education (1991). *County system review.* Edmonton Regional Office.

Fullan, M. (1988). *What's worth fighting for in the principalship?* Toronto: Ontario Public School Teachers' Federation.

Hall, G., Hord, S., Rutherford, W. & Huling, L. (1984). Change in high schools: Rolling stones or asleep at the wheel? *Educational Leadership, 41,* 58-62.

Hallinger, P., Bickman, L. & Davis, K. (1989). *What makes a difference? School context, principal leadership and student achievement.* Paper presented at the annual meeting of the American Educational Research Association, San Francisco, March.

Saskatchewan Educational Leadership Unit (1990). *Planning for the 1990's* (A study for a school division). College of Education, University of Saskatchewan, Saskatoon.

# SECTION THREE

# Vision and Vitality

In this section a shift is made from emphasis on voices to connecting what has been said in the internal analysis to the outcomes of the environmental scan. Such integration is demanding yet exciting. This is the part of strategic planning where leaders together with partners in education put the pieces together so that alternate futures for the school system begin to take shape and a preferred future is shared and put forward. It is this vision of a preferred future that focuses attention, energizes change processes, provides meaning for individual daily efforts and directs evaluation. It is the vision and strong leadership that provide vitality.

# 7

# Leadership—Visioning and Sharing

*Our particular school is being run in a helter-skelter
manner . . . a real lack of direction is apparent.*

- a teacher

Leaders? Who are they? President Bush? Audrey McLaughlin, the first woman to lead a federal party in Canada? President Gorbachev? Mother Theresa? Bennis (1990) claims that since Martin Luther King and John F. Kennedy there has been a lack of leadership in the United States. Churchill is generally considered to have been a great wartime leader who did not do as well in peacetime. What characteristics do we see in people whom we consider leaders? Martin Luther King spoke with such feeling of his dream—vision seems to be an attribute. Churchill could rally a country with eloquent, pounding speeches—persuasion and passion we could say. They seem to know what they believe and take strong positions yet relate to others with openness, honesty and integrity—think of Mother Theresa. There is also a sense of giving, it seems, as we think of John F. Kennedy, independently wealthy, who implored Americans to think more of what they could give to their country than what they could get from it. Yes, some characteristics do seem to stand out in national and international leaders —vision and persuasion among them.

## What is Leadership?

Our dictionary defines a leader as a directing, commanding or guiding head of a group or activity. We generally use the word "command" and "commander" in relation to a military context. Some leaders in education are called "directors" and others "superintendents"—think of what these words imply. Do we have a language problem? The only "guides" we can think of are Girl Guides and those who help us through the wilderness or to find fish in a lake, yet the word is closer to describing leaders in current educational contexts than director or commander. A leader was portrayed as someone at the centre of a web, rather than at the top of a hierarchy, in a book on women in leadership by Helgesen (1990).

Most people describe a leader as someone who is at the head of a group or responsible for an activity—out in front. Examples considered earlier as well as literature indicate that such people frequently are characterized by vision—seeing how things could be better, and persuasion—human relations skills.

Looking more formally at studies of leadership in education, early attempts were directed at studying traits of leaders in terms of physical appearance and background. A current approach relates gender to leadership style. Many readers will have considered situational leadership literature which draws attention to the task, the group and power as determinants of what is appropriate leadership style. We have all observed political leaders who are relatively successful at a particular time in a certain context and less successful on other occasions in other places. Studies and observations of situational factors affecting leadership have utility in education, too: a superintendent is more directive in dealing with sexual harassment than in the implementation of whole language; a principal relates differently to experienced teachers considering program continuity than he does in preparing new teachers for a fire drill. More recent work by Sergiovanni (1984) is receiving increased attention as calls for leadership in education mount. He outlines five leadership forces:

1. Cultural—building a strong organizational culture (articulating purposes, reinforcing beliefs, rewarding, explaining "how we do things around here"),

2. Symbolic—focusing attention on what is most important (vision and persuasion),

3. Educational—expertise in curriculum, supervision, etc.,

4. Human—encouraging, supporting, getting along well, and

5. Technical—managing timetables, budgets, supplies, etc.

Sergiovanni believes that a leader can have a competent school with technical, human and educational forces but that excellence requires the impact of symbolic and cultural dimensions. In other words, we "can keep the ship afloat" by applying the first three leadership forces—some call this "managing." If we want it to move in certain directions, symbolic and cultural leadership forces have to be present—that is leadership. Some refer to some schools as dead or stuck and others as growing and moving. If you think of schools you know, into which category would they fall?

## Why is Leadership Difficult?

If learning and growing and moving are so natural and basic to living, why is leadership to facilitate these processes so difficult? Some of the stumbling blocks are related to human frailty, some to social conditions and some to characteristics of educational organizations.

While change is exciting and potentially satisfying to people, it also increases uncertainty and inevitably brings about some anxiety. Consider, for example, a summer holiday at your cottage compared to a trip to France—something new. Old shoes are usually more comfortable than new shoes. People for good reason have a natural resistance to someone who tries to get them to do something differently. This makes leadership difficult.

At this time in history in many countries there is general disillusionment with political and religious leaders particularly. Cases of sexual abuse, conflict of interest and patronage receive more attention in the media than they should. In the 1980s courts seem to have become more influential than legislatures. Events in Eastern Europe have resulted more from mass demonstrations than from leadership. Leaders on this continent appeared to wait for public opinion polls to support a clean air bill before they acted. Teachers have seen "hot shot" superintendents come in with bright ideas, stir things up and then leave before their efforts bear fruit. When confronted with the "push" of the next superintendent they don't get too excited, thinking "This too shall pass." For many reasons leadership in our society at this time is a major challenge, yet the need has never been greater. Public expectations continue to soar.

School organizations are peculiar compared to business and industrial enterprises. They have been "domesticated" in that they have not had to compete for survival. This is beginning to change somewhat but schools have survived whether they were good, bad or otherwise. Schools also have traditionally had multiple and unclear goals compared to other organizations. It is, therefore, much more difficult for a school principal than it is for a bank manager to decide if it has been a "good day." A further complication in most schools is that they are "loose"—efforts are not co-ordinated, individuals work in isolation and supervision/evaluation causes considerable difficulty. Teachers have had a "pocket veto" to close their classroom door, do as they wish and let the leader whistle!

A final point is what we see as a lack of respect for leadership in schooling particularly in sparsely populated areas. Some facts will illustrate: A relatively small Saskatchewan city has an elected school board of 7 members; 20 000 students; 1 200 teachers and 75 people in leadership positions (central office and supervising principals). Also in Saskatchewan, a rural school system has 52 elected local trustees and system board members; 1 200 students, 82 teachers and one person in a full-time leadership position—the superintendent. Consider the urban-rural differences in ratio of board members to students, teachers and leadership positions. Economic hardship has resulted in central office staff being reduced in many small school systems. Efforts to have three or four teachers/principals per year rotated into central leadership positions have failed because the classroom teachers think only classroom teachers really count in the total scheme of things. This is what we mean by lack of respect for leadership and it is a very serious problem in many small school systems. It also has to be said that some school boards do not want a leader—they want someone who will "play it safe," so they can be reelected.

Most readers will have had experience in confronting factors which make leadership difficult. Yet leadership is like life—it may be difficult but it is better than the alternative! The world is not going to get any less complex nor leadership any less difficult. Our response must be to extend our understanding of leadership, improve our skills, review priorities, strengthen networks and increase our resolve.

> *Leaders should do the leading. We have too*
> *many committees and too many meetings.*
>
> - a teacher

## Visioning

**Meaning.** We are convinced that vision is a central and crucial aspect of leadership. It may be thought of as moral imagination—picturing how things could be better. Vision starts from within and is personal. It is something we care deeply about. We may have a picture of an ideal marital relationship or an adequate savings plan. We may have visions during illness of what it will be like to feel well again. Most of us imagine what a board meeting could be like if only one troublesome member should not be reelected. The point is that visions are specific and concrete. They are more specific and realistic than dreams. They are more concrete than purposes although they reflect an underlying purpose. Examples of vision are having a man on the moon by 1970, paying off the mortgage in five years, implementing an integrated curriculum in three years or having principals become instructional leaders in two years. A vision is a destination—a desired future. In a changing world, in keeping with the spirit of this book, a vision is continually refined and refocused but we must persist —we care enough to commit ourselves to it and to make some sacrifice to achieve it. So far we are talking about personal vision. Where do you see your school system in three years in relation to those aspects you care most about?

**Formulating a Vision.** Education should be future oriented because the most important people in the business are students whose life is about 80 percent in the future. Surveys and dialogue indicate that the public would like schools to place more emphasis on the future. Our society is compelled to do this because of increasing concerns about the impact of our lifestyle on the environment, world food supply, health costs and quality of life in general. Another compelling reason for more emphasis on vision—desired futures—is illustrated in Figure 7.1. Typically, when the public is disenchanted with schools as they are, they have only one alternative view of schools as they were when they attended decades ago. So we, not surprisingly, hear calls for "back to the basics." Generally we have failed as leaders to put alternative futures of schooling before the public for consideration. This type of scenario construction may be started with analysis of available information to search for trends. For example, if enrolment trends continue, if teachers retire at the usual time, and if government priorities remain constant what will the picture be in five years? This would be the most likely scenario. From that it is not difficult, on the basis of partners' voices, to discuss and picture the best that could happen and the worst that could happen. Could a new mine open? Is the natural farming movement likely to flourish resulting in more intensive agriculture? Are more adults likely to enrol in continuing education? Could the school really become involved in community development? May the Indian people withdraw their children to a reserve school? What is the potential of distance education? The construction of scenarios is where community people particularly have much to contribute. It is where leaders take personal positions, share their vision and work closely with others to focus discussion of alternative scenarios on a preferred future shared by all—an articulated and shared vision. Such a vision has the power to focus the talents and energy of all concerned in moving in directions which have been agreed upon. It helps to create a sense of community as it involves both the head and the heart.

Figure 7.1
Views of Schools

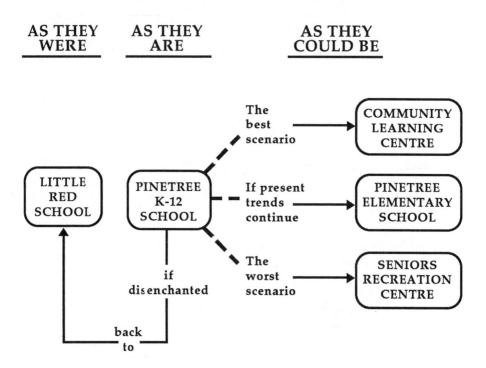

*We work really well together—the three of us. Like we're going
out on a camp to send the kids off—a sort of farewell from the school.*
- a beginning teacher

**Guidelines and Pitfalls**. There are current studies and conversations
about the construction of meaning from the learners' perspective, education program continuity and generally focusing on learning and teaching
to help students see how things are interrelated. This integration is equally
important for all of us but particularly for leaders in schooling. Seeing
connections makes life meaningful. At this point we need to emphasize
that the external analysis and internal analysis of the strategic planning
approach are integrated through leadership, dialogue and an articulated,
shared vision. Once a vision is "up front," we can design programs and
policies so that all those involved have a sense of direction and a sense of
community. The gap between "what is" and a realistic vision is motivating.
It creates a healthy tension. Moreover, daily efforts can be seen in relation
to the vision and thus become meaningful. The guidelines we offer are as
follows:

1. There is no substitute for the leader who is aware of the bigger picture, who sees how parts are interrelated, who can tol-
   erate ambiguity and who is committed to her/his own
   lifelong learning.

2. The importance of leaders thinking deeply and formulating
   personal visions cannot be over-emphasized. This is the starting point for articulating and sharing a vision.

3. A "top down" vision statement or seeing a vision as a solu-
   tion to a problem is not likely to be very useful. People will
   not "take it to heart."

4. Leaders must keep visions "up front" by focussing attention
   towards its realization and by helping people to find meaning in their day-to-day efforts—enabling them to see how
   they are connected to directions in which the school system is
   moving.

5. Fundamental to visioning is integrity and a high level of
   human relations skills. Several writers are using the term
   "thoughtfulness" and we know of at least one rural school
   system that has made thoughtfulness central to their entire

operation. We are not playing games. Schooling is serious
business. We must be sincere in our efforts to give partners a
voice and to listen—to be thoughtful—realizing that this may
result in a change of our personal position/vision. We have
to open and bring our own deep beliefs and assumptions to
the surface so people will understand our position and so
that we too may learn and grow.

We do not want to preach in elaborating these points but we care deeply
about the directions we see many schools moving particularly in sparsely
populated areas. In many ways they are like the communities they serve
—declining. There do seem to be feelings of disillusionment, of being stuck
and thinking "There is nothing we can do." We have seen vision statements
formulated with good intentions from "on high" but little happening as a
result. The good news is that in similar circumstances some people do "get
it all together" culminating in a vision statement which energizes all
concerned—the school "takes off." Most of our guidelines are based on
what we have learned from those people. We have our personal vision of
effective schools in sparsely populated areas.

## Leadership as a Quality of Organizations

Schools in sparsely populated areas have always been vulnerable to
having leaders move away. Recent views of leadership as a quality of
organizations, supported by our experience in seeing it happen, should
offer new hope for continuity of leadership.

Earlier we traced leadership studies from concentration on personal
traits, then situations to more recent views of technical, human, educational, symbolic and cultural forces. Personal traits no doubt enter the
picture and we have all, intuitively or otherwise, adapted our leadership
behaviour to particular situations. We are convinced that much more
emphasis needs to be given to symbolic and cultural forces which will
result in vision, focused attention, energy, meaning and improved learning. Another major outcome is that the processes we are advocating will
build leadership into the organization. The vision in a learning organization does not depend upon an individual: if we hear partners' voices once
they will expect to be involved again in the not too distant future; if school
and community groups get into genuine dialogue which extends
everyone's learning they will want to continue; if people once have a sense
of direction they will feel lost without it; and if communication has helped
people find meaning in daily work they will not want to lose it. Organizations, in the final analysis, are people, and leadership can be built through

people into the overriding strategic planning process. All other endeavors of parents, boards, teachers and administrators are related to that process.

Does this sound far-fetched? Recall that we have highlighted the moral imagination (seeing how things could be better—vision) and human relations components of leadership. Once people engage in a continual process of linking external conditions and internal analysis to directions for the school we can see that leadership will come from many sources and that the human relations skills of everyone will improve. There will be many ideas from various perspectives regarding how the school could be better. The overall strategic planning process will have communication channels, forums for dialogue and decision-making strategies built into the organization so that ideas and energy, from whatever source, can be of maximum benefit to the school. These processes become a central part of the school culture—"how we do things around here." Just let a newcomer focus only on management or try a "top down" style!

Our experience, our reading and our dialogue have convinced us that women in leadership positions typically adopt a style that is conducive to the creation of learning organizations. For years we have worked closely with women who are consultants, principals, superintendents, deputy ministers, ministers, deans, university presidents and school board chairs. We have seen them consistently work according to principles identified in Helgesen's book, *The Female Advantage: Women's Ways of Leadership* (1990). These principles include focus on the big picture (vision), emphasis on networks instead of hierarchy, expressions of inclusion, caring, listening and integrating professional and personal life. These qualities may account for growing numbers of women in leadership roles and for Naisbitt and Aburdene, in *Megatrends 2000*, giving a chapter the title, "The 1990's: Decade of Women in Leadership."

## Turning to Illustrations

Illustrations given in preceding chapters reflect leadership views of "how things could be better" and human relations skills to bring about related action. Various leaders have had visions related to school-community development, student involvement, parent participation and support for teachers. Readers will be able to think of other examples of leadership from various levels of school organizations and we invite you to record some thoughts at the end of this section. We share some illustrations below.

A principal in Calingiri Elementary School, Western Australia, had an idea to enrich learning and to bring the school and community closer together. Under his leadership the grade 6 and 7 students researched, wrote and presented the history of a winery associated with a nearby monastery. Each of the students had a voice part on a video that was produced. The outcomes included a state award for innovation.

People at the Mid-continent Regional Educational Laboratory (McREL) believed that various efforts of reform in education would be better if there was a system that incorporated reform, redesign and restructuring. The result has been A+chieving Excellence, a new framework for managing school improvement. McREL staff offer three-day institutes to prepare staff for ongoing attention to efficiency, effectiveness and excellence in their schools. Related materials are available by calling McREL in Aurora, Colorado at (303) 337-0990.

There was a felt need in North Dakota for more participation in deciding directions for education. The North Dakota Education Action Commission was established to represent a wide range of perspectives. It worked for months to prepare a document for discussion at eight public hearings across the state. The document is said to be only one part of an evolving process to build basic agreement regarding the direction of public education in the state.

Leaders in the Lanigan School Division in Saskatchewan had a vision of a "school of the future" that would better meet the needs of its students in preparing for the next century. The vision has become a reality through hiring a consultant to prepare a proposal, a needs assessment, acquisition of external funding from a future corporation and from business and industry and an extensive professional development program. The school features computers for students, distance education, partnerships with industry, work experience, co-operative education, guidance, career planning and counselling. In addition there is emphasis on lifelong learning, adult upgrading and networks with other schools.

The County of Wheatland in central Alberta emphasizes participation. The superintendent believed that the system would be better with more student involvement and better communication. Each year students from secondary schools have a simulated school board meeting during Education Week and there is also another such meeting for parents. Current issues are placed on the agenda for students and parents. The feedback is seen as useful by the board. Also each year in early December parents, teachers and students come together for "Think Tank Sessions." The ideas generated are passed along to school administrators and trustees who have a two-day workshop to formulate objectives and action plans for the coming school year.

In the Kerrobert School Division in Saskatchewan, a provincial school improvement model with related resources has been linked to initiatives at the school-community level in such a way that several features of a learning organization have been developed. During interviews the 10 teachers of the grades 7 to 12 school attributed success to leadership, collaboration, shared decision making, early success, staff stability and a reasonable pace of change. When asked if the improvement process would continue if key advocates were to leave the general reaction is captured in the following response: "Oh, yes. We have lots of ideas for improving this school and now that we are used to working together (the project started in 1986) we would have it no other way."

The best current example of leadership for schooling that I can think of is . . .

## Summary

We fully expect that many readers are already working very effectively at high levels of leadership. What we have written will have confirmed and supported what is underway. We simply ask if, in case you leave, you are building leadership into your organization. We ask also if women are supported in assuming and exercising leadership.

Some may be overloaded and bogged down with managerial tasks. You may not feel like a leader. Unless someone in the system is leading, your schools are likely "stuck." Individual teachers may be very effective and some schools may have a unifying vision but without system integration and support these efforts are "hit and miss" and very vulnerable to political influence and/or personnel changes. There is no assurance of continuity of quality education and rural people deserve better than that.

If you are not doing what you would like to do as a leader we suggest that you reflect on your personal beliefs, analyze the context in which you are working (listen to the voices), decide on one or two aspects that you care most about and then picture how things might get better in those areas. Determine your position. Share it. Listen and act. You may decide, for example, to advocate additional support for the library, an exchange program with urban students or a school-community effort to increase awareness of drug and alcohol abuse. You will have taken a stand and accepted responsibility. You will "feel like a leader"—the first step in being one.

*The principals basically run their schools. They have the most control over their schools. They seem happy that we are involving them a little more.*

- a trustee

## References

Bermis, W. (1990). *Why leaders can't lead: The unconscious conspiracy continues.* San Francisco: Jossey-Bass.

Helgesen, S. (1990). *The female advantage: Women's ways of leadership.* Toronto: Doubleday Currency.

Naisbitt, J. & Aburdene, P. (1990). *Megatrends 2000: Ten new directions for the 1990's.* New York: Avon Books.

Ogawa, R. & Bossert, S. (1989). *Leadership as an organizational quality.* A paper presented at the annual meeting of the American Educational Research Association, San Francisco, March.

Senge, P. (1990). *The fifth discipline: The art and practice of the learning organization.* Toronto: Doubleday Currency.

Sergiovanni, T. (1984). *Leadership and excellence in schooling.* Educational Leadership, 41(5), 4-13.

# 8

# Change Processes in Education

*Change is very hard to achieve in a rural*
*school because the community resists it.*

- a teacher

The Chinese character for change is made up of two parts: one means "risk" and the other "opportunity." These are no doubt the feelings we have experienced as we met new friends, bought a new boat or moved into a new community. It is important for us to reflect on our personal experiences with change as a way to gain insight into how to lead change processes in schools. Since change has been, and will be, an important part of our personal and professional/business life it is important to understand its basic features.

 In relation to strategic planning, change means moving from "what is" to what is visioned as a desired future. It is "getting from here to there." In this chapter the meaning of change will be reviewed, phases will be described and three examples will be presented. Finally, key considerations for leaders in sparsely populated areas will be put forward.

## Change

### Meaning

The theme of Michael Fullan's book, *The New Meaning of Educational Change* (1991), is that we must pay more attention to what a particular change means to the people who have to implement it as compared to meaning it had for the people who came up with or developed the idea. For example, governments, telephone companies and computer experts may work together to make distance education available to small schools —great, but what will it mean to students, classroom teachers, principals and the local community? Typically such a change for teachers would mean a different role with students, use of new learning resources in the classroom and reexamination of what they had always considered to be quality education. Integration of handicapped students into regular classrooms has usually meant that school board members have had to gain more knowledge, spend more money and take some criticism from the community. All of this is part of the subjective meaning of change as are more work, some threat, periods of anxiety, challenge and excitement —the risks and the opportunities. The objective meaning of change is that in the minds of those who promote the change and it usually appears on paper. We do not need to be reminded of the differences between what is written and what is done! It is important to realize, however, that any change will have greatly different meanings among any group of people.

*The exam is identical to the one I had when I was a student.*

- a parent

### Phases

Margaret Thatcher resigned at 9:00 a.m. on November 22, 1990. Marriages take place at certain hours on certain days. There is a tendency to think that change is an event, but it is not. It is a process. In the two examples above, a change in leadership and the marriage of people, the change became official at a point in time but both are processes with many "ups and downs" over long periods of time. Change in education is also a process, not an event. Distance education may be "hooked up" at a particular moment but it will be two or three years before it is fully utilized as intended.

The change process in education is commonly considered to have phases of adoption, implementation and institutionalization or continuation. Although teachers are primarily involved in implementation, each phase deserves some elaboration since they are interdependent and include both patterns and the unexpected.

The *adoption phase* is "change on paper." A government may decide to consolidate school systems or to require sex education. A school division may have a board vote on hiring a counsellor. A school staff may decide to give priority to resource-based learning. Adoption, the first step in the change process, is affected by many factors including socio-political conditions, school and system characteristics, and underlying values and beliefs. The need for lifelong learning in the next century is one factor which is affecting the adoption of many new courses of study. What do you think has influenced the adoption of new policy/programs by your government or school board?

Adoption is only a beginning. The phase of change which is much more complicated is *implementation*—"making it happen" as intended. Readers, no doubt, can reflect on many experiences they have had in trying to bring about change in a school. Can you list some factors which facilitated the process and some which presented barriers? Below is a list of considerations which often affect implementation:

1. Characteristics of the change itself—Is it needed? Is the meaning clear? Are related materials readily available? Is it of high quality? Is it practical?

2. School system characteristics—Is the superintendent a strong advocate? Has money been made available? Is there ongoing opportunity for professional development and follow-up? Is there a reasonable time line for implementation (three years or so)? Does anyone care if it happens? Will there be monitoring and evaluation?

3. Features of the school—Is the change clearly a priority of the principal? Is it linked to the vision and goals of the school? Do the teachers talk to one another about it? Is the school climate supportive when things do not go well? Is decision making shared? Do teachers see one another "in action" through peer coaching, developmental supervision, etc.?

4. Societal considerations—Is the government likely to maintain support for this change? Will declining enrolments or changing student population make a difference? Is the community conservative or futuristic (do parents want students to have a spelling list every Friday)? Are there good school-community relations?

As you decide whether your response to each question is a facilitating factor or a barrier, which list is longer? The challenge in planning for implementation is to build upon the positive factors and to take steps to reduce the negative impact of, or overcome, the barriers. We are not yet finished! It has been found in formal studies as well as in experience that factors interact and shift over time. School culture, professional development activities and teacher interaction patterns affect each other. The principal may be strongly supportive early in the implementation and neglect the process later on. Implementation is clearly a challenge and an adventure.

There is another aspect of implementation that needs to be emphasized. We often think a change is either implemented or it is not but it is not an "either-or" question. Teachers in the case of curriculum change, for example, have been found to move through stages of concern as they attain different levels of use (see, for example, Hall, Loucks et al, 1975). The process is not straightforward but the idea of moving from concern about yourself, to worries about the change and then to what difference it makes, seems to make sense to most people. In a new situation we tend to be worried about "How will I do?" Later we concentrate on the substance of the change and the impact. Similarly levels of use typically are labelled as non-use, information, preparation, routine use, integration, refinement and renewal. People of course move along levels at different rates and also fall back at times. The point to remember is that making a change is not like flicking a light switch. There are stages of thinking it over, getting ready, trying it out, taking some more steps, checking the results and making it better. People at any one time will be at different stages of concern and levels of use whether we are talking about teachers implementing a new curriculum, new board members getting used to their duties or a community adjusting to school closure.

For implementation to be successful a leader must orchestrate the interaction of many factors as the picture changes from week to week in any school-community. Have you had, or do you presently have, such a role?

*Continuation* of a change should not be taken for granted. It, too, depends upon a host of factors including the processes of adoption and implementation. Many changes, such as integrated curriculum or a non-graded organization of schools never achieve higher than a routine level of implementation. Some changes such as open-area classrooms are clearly discontinued as walls are constructed. Studies also reveal that changes such as outdoor education and use of technology often decline rapidly when key supporters leave the school. Staff changes and political factors typically threaten many innovations. Another difficulty is that monitoring and evaluation aspects of change processes are usually neglected, resulting in an inadequate base of information upon which to make decisions for continuation.

The foregoing description of change is based upon studies of school systems. To illustrate how various factors emerge, three recent studies are summarized.

## Cases

The first case, Eastview, focuses on factors which affected a new superintendent's efforts to be a leader. The second, Rose Valley, is a report of the meaning of a provincially-mandated instructional change to teachers in early stages of implementation. A longitudinal study of multiple changes in Parkland School Divisions is reviewed as the third example. The first two cases are drawn from unpublished graduate work at the University of Saskatchewan. Anyone wishing to have a more complete report could contact the authors. The Parkland case is reported in more detail in an article by Earle Newton in *Research in Rural Education*, fall, 1990.

## Eastview

The focus of this case study was the determination and analysis of factors affecting the leadership of a superintendent new to a rural school system of 2 146 students, 134 teachers and 10 schools. Eastview was growing slowly due to an agricultural base, a potash industry and proximity to a city. The communities within the system varied greatly in terms of culture, tradition and expectations. Families ranged from river estates to "squatters." For the first time in 14 years the 7 elected board members had to search for a new superintedent. They went about it carefully and consulted widely in deciding on a selection process. They concluded that they wanted someone who was a strong leader to initiate policy development within the system, to supervise and evaluate teachers and to launch various professional development programs. They also decided to give priority to someone who was computer literate and knowledgeable in the arts. An interview and assessment form were used in the final stages of the process. Thus, Mr. Strong was selected on his condition that the role of chief executive officer be evaluated by the Board annually.

Since that time a mission statement and slogan "Seeking Excellence through Service and Dedication" has been highlighted. According to interview data, the Superintedent's vision and values are reflected in those initiatives. Other changes include decentralized budgets, yearly Board-administrator retreats, increased visibility of the Superintendent, emphasis on supervision and evaluation of teachers, mandated yearly plans by teachers and several teacher task forces.

Mr. Strong is perceived to be inflexible once a decision has been made to pursue a particular course of action. He did not back off in the face of teacher opposition to submitting long-range plans to the principal and central office. Two principals were demoted.

On the basis of interviews with board members, central office personnel, in-school administrators and teachers the factors shown in Table 8.1 have been identified as affecting Mr. Strong's performance as a leader. It was revealed in these data that Mr. Strong is viewed as tough and inflexible at times. Many individuals also attested to his compassion and understanding in personal matters and to his "soft spot" for children. He is also credited with guiding the Board in achieving what it wanted to do and in improving its public image. He is reported to have given the term "instructional leadership" meaning within the school system. It is said that Mr. Strong has given the system a vision. He claims that he is not a gifted person but that he surrounds himself with talented people who share his visions.

### Table 8.1 Factors Affecting Mr. Strong's Effectiveness as a Leader

| | Facilitators | | Barriers |
|---|---|---|---|
| 1. | System size: numbers workable, personalized | 1. | System size: small K-12 schools, limited offerings |
| 2. | Location: near a city, many applications for positions | 2. | Location: communities far apart, losing students to city system |
| 3. | Superintendent: role model, (hard work, dedication) | 3. | Economic hardship: lower grant increases, poor rural conditions |
| 4. | School facilities: gyms, resource centres etc. | 4. | Superintendent: seen as controlling, away from the system for outside commitments |
| 5. | School Board: willing to lead, supportive, hardworking | 5. | Change slow and difficult, unable to opt out |
| 6. | Central office personnel: team approach | 6. | Lack of communication with the broader community |
| 7. | Successful implementation of provincially mandated instructional changes | 7. | Lack of clear direction regarding government mandates/priorities |
| 8. | Staff: dedicated, willing to meet challenges | 8. | Staff: preference for the status quo |
| 9. | Schools: goal focused, climate, staff development | | |
| 10. | Supervision/Evaluation: growth in monitoring | | |
| 11. | Teacher transfers to experience new environments | | |

## Rose Valley

The setting is a rural school system in a mixed farming area. The 983 students attended one of nine schools in five communities and three Hutterite colonies. The seven-member elected school board employed 62 full-time teachers, 11 part-time teachers, a superintendent and support staff. The Superintendent, formerly principal of a grade 7-12 school in the main town, had been in his position for eight years. The study was concentrated on four, K-12 schools with 37 teachers among them where the implementation of a provincially mandated instructional change was at the end of its second year. The innovation, known as Common Essential Learnings (CELs), was to incorporate six "threads" into all subjects at all grade levels. The learnings were: communication; numeracy; critical and creative thinking; technological literacy; personal and social values and skills; independent learning. The expectation was that each teacher would make specific, deliberate efforts to integrate these learnings into their teaching. Support for teachers included print materials from government, a regional co-ordinator and four professional development days.

The general purpose of the study was to investigate how teachers develop commitment to an innovation which is in early stages of implementation. Special attention was given to the meaning of the change, teacher interaction patterns and how teachers fit the new approach into what they had been used to doing. Data were collected by means of questionnaires to all teachers, interviews with three or four professional staff in each school, print materials and visits to each school.

Findings from the study are as follows:

1. Implementation activities varied greatly from school to school even within this same system.

2. School differences can be attributed primarily to the interest of the principal. Teacher implementation teams had little effect.

3. Teachers generally had very limited knowledge and understanding of the Common Essential Learnings. Thus, they did not talk to one another much about it.

4. A lack of visible leadership from the Superintendent resulted in teachers not knowing what was expected of them and wondering if anyone really cared about the implementation.

5.Teachers usually had their professional development occur away from their school where they could meet people teaching at their grade level. They preferred practical experiences and discussion with peers.

6. Leadership, if any, came from teachers of high school grades or the principal.

The implications of this study for leaders of small schools are numerous. The first is that teachers require sustained pressure (clear goals and expectations) and support from the system level if change processes are to be successful. A second implication is that teachers need more opportunities to have interaction with colleagues from other schools since school level professional development was virtually non-existent. A third implication is that simply having teacher groups or committees is not enough—they too require a balance of pressure and support.

This study revealed that even an intuitively appealing innovation designed to prepare students for lifelong learning, mandated by government, supported with considerable time for professional development and with provision for teacher groups to offer leadership "did not really happen" at the classroom level after two years. Lack of leadership at the system level, virtually no related professional development at the school level and very limited teacher interaction stalled the implementation of a major provincial curriculum change.

## Parkland

Reviewed here is a five-year study of Parkland School Division which covers approximately 1 500 square miles in a remote area of east, central Saskatchewan. Most people are descendants of Ukrainian settlers who came at the turn of the century to begin mixed-farming. The area has experienced enrolment decline from a high of about 1 800 students to the current 1 300. These students attend 10 schools in 8 communities served by 85 teachers and a superintendent. There are 44 elected local board members and 6 elected system board members.

In 1982 a planning study of the school system was done to provide base-line information for dialogue and long-range planning. Concerns at the time centred around enrolment decline, school closure, finance and student transportation. During the study it was learned that students, teachers and parents had many ideas for improving the program and the operation of the schools.

After the 1982 study many changes came about. With the support of a government educational development fund, itinerant teachers were hired for special education, education for the gifted and science in small schools. In addition, a person was hired to act as liaison with an Indian band on an adjacent reserve. A work-study program was started and a developmental centre for the educable mentally retarded was incorporated into one of the schools. The Superintendent took a special interest in computer-related programs and these were introduced into schools. There was a series of ten video-centred professional development programs pertaining to the integration of special needs students. In addition, an administrative leadership development program was conducted with principals during 1985-86.

In 1986 a second study was conducted to document school improvements underway, to determine whether or not programs adopted were being implemented (reaching the students), to identify factors affecting change processes and to gain insight into how multiple changes are managed in diverse school-communities within one school system. Data were gathered by means of questionnaires to all students in grades 7 to 12 and to all teachers. All professional staff were interviewed, documents were reviewed and meetings were attended.

Findings were encouraging in that teachers believed that Board initiatives were making a difference to students. The greatest gains in program profiles were in the areas of computers and special education. Teachers did not report as much progress in science, second languages or provincially mandated curriculum changes.

Teachers most frequently drew support from their own professional preparation, teacher choice of methods and materials and extra hours of preparation. The services providing the least support were the system student assessment program, community resources (field trips, etc.), librarians and resource teachers, shared planning by teachers and teachers' influence on system policy. Teachers were very appreciative of opportunities for in-service programs which averaged support for each teacher to attend one workshop per year outside of the school system in addition to systemwide and school activities. When teachers were asked to indicate the sources of support they drew upon specifically to implement new programs in order of frequency they listed the Superintendent, teachers' informal discussions, related resource materials, workshops, parents and community, discussions with the principal and itinerant teachers. Major difficulties reported by teachers were that everything seemed to be "added on" and not integrated, that there was difficulty in getting new learning materials and the general problem of work overload. Most teachers believed that they were more effective in 1986 than they had been in 1982, and that they were supported in a process of on-going professional development.

By way of summary several points should be made:

1. Changes were adopted as a result of the interaction among socio-political, financial and organizational factors. Included was the availability of external resources for a planning study, "seed money" from government, ideas for program change from several perspectives within the system, a changing, more open school board and a particularly alert and dedicated superintendent. Enrolment decline sparked the whole process.

2. Teachers derived more support from their own resources and the school system than they did from school-community factors.

3. Full implementation and continuation of the changes were threatened by worsening economic conditions, retrenching by the Board into local as compared to system perspectives and lack of integrated, continuous support for teachers from all levels of the system.

## Key Considerations

The three cases are interesting because the change in Eastview is continuing, the Rose Valley implementation has not yet happened – so far it is a non-event, and most of the multiple changes in Parkland are seriously threatened. Several key considerations surface:

1. The impetus for the three changes can be attributed to a combination of factors including competition from a neighbouring city system, a provincial mandate and declining enrolments. Large schools and mixed communities often generate enough conflict to initiate change processes but small schools in homogenous communities may lack a spark to get change underway. That is why it is important to clearly determine gaps between reality and vision which will likely motivate people to take action.

2. The Eastview case illustrates that even with a board mandate for change, a strong leader, some competition for students and quality staff, change is slow and difficult.

3. It should also be noted that the Eastview superintendent was strong in at least two respects: he had a vision which was communicated and shared; he did not back down when teachers resisted but helped to some extent in early stages of a change process. (Do you remember getting used to bifocals or trying a new grip on a golf club?)

4. Teacher interaction patterns within the school emerged in the Rose Valley and Parkland contexts as barriers to change. The teachers derived support primarily from their own sources or from networks with colleagues in other schools. School level leadership and professional development were weak in both situations. These and other studies indicate that it is a mistake to assume that staffs in small schools support each other in, or even talk about, efforts to bring about improvement in the school.

5. If we consider three levels of school organization to be school, system and province/state, there must be an integrated and continuous balance of pressure and support at all levels. In Eastview, system and school initiatives were hampered by lack of clarity at the level of government, Rose Valley had only government leadership and Parkland lacked school level involvement.

6. Barriers to implementation of change and threats to continuation certainly do appear. Only in Eastview was there any indication of leadership being built into the organization as a safeguard against threats.

*Policy is useful sometimes in a political sense to get you off the hook."*
- a trustee

These three cases and other references listed at the end of the chapter make it vividly clear that change processes in education are intriguing. They are both simple and complex. They involve both global and personal factors. Orchestrating interacting factors which affect change processes over time requires leadership of the highest calibre. It involves a combination of knowledge, familiarity with a particular context, intuition and a "feel" for the improvement process.

> *This is a really good staff to work with. They're really good —really supportive and you need that. "*
> - a beginning teacher

## References

Casswell-Beckmann, J. (1989). *Instructional leadership of a director: A vision for the future*. Unpublished paper, College of Education, University of Saskatchewan, Saskatoon.

Dibski, D., Newton, E & Sackney, L. (1990). *Integration of theory and practice in rural schools through a provincial leadership unit*. Paper presented at the annual meeting of the American Educational Research Association, Boston, April.

Fullan, M. (1991). *The new meaning of educational change*. Toronto: OISE Press.

Fullan, M., Anderson, S. & Newton, E. (1986). *Support systems for implementing curriculum in school boards*. Toronto: OISE Press.

Gulka, W. (1990). *Curriculum implementation and teacher commitment*. Unpublished M.Ed. thesis, University of Saskatchewan, Saskatoon.

Hall, G., Loucks, S., Rutherford, W. & Newlove, B. (1975). Levels of use of the innovation: A framework for analyzing innovation adoption. *Journal of Teacher Education, 26*(1), 52-56.

Newton, E. (1989). *Innovations in secondary schools: Problems and possibilities for the 1990's*. A paper presented at an international conference on school-based innovations, Hong Kong, December.

Newton, E. (1990). Rural teachers' perceptions of support for program change. *Research in rural education, 7*(1), 42-54.

Newton, E. (1990). Why are we here? A five-year study of institutional development in a secondary school. *School Organization, 10*(1), 139-154.

Newton, E. (1990). *Implementation of a provincial school improvement program: Problems and possibilities for 2020*. A paper presented at a conference "Facing the Challenge: School Year 2020" sponsored by International Movements Toward Educational Change (IMTEC), Oxford, England, September.

Newton, E. & Wright, R. (1987). Forces affecting change in small rural schools. *School Organization, 7*(3), 357-366.

# 9

## Monitoring and Evaluation

*We don't see superintendents very often. We need*
*feedback from them on how the school is doing.*

- representative comment of school staff

This chapter gives monitoring and evaluation particular attention for two reasons. Firstly, they are an integral part of two strong characteristics of our society—information and accountability. Secondly, monitoring and evaluation are problematic aspects of strategic planning and are, therefore, often neglected in school organizations. For our purposes we shall think of monitoring as systematically collecting information about the performance of a school or school system. Evaluation is a judgment on the basis of the information collected. These terms will be elaborated upon in sections which follow. First it is important to recognize that monitoring and evaluation present major challenges to leaders for schooling.

## Background

This period in our history is accurately and commonly referred to as the information age. We are bombarded with facts and figures about the environment, trade, the economy, businesses, new cars and even the performance of our entertainers and athletes. At times we feel an information overload yet it is generally recognized that information is power. Writers such as Carkhuff (1988) talk of information capital and illustrate that enterprises with complete, relevant information are more successful and, therefore, worth more than their competitors. A farmer considering whether or not to go into raising hogs needs detailed information, not only about his present grain farm, but also about breeds of pigs, hog barns, nutrition, health care for animals, and markets including changing public attitudes toward consumption of pork. Similar information would be needed about the possibility of raising cattle, sheep or chickens so that a sound decision could be made. The quality of information collected would determine, to a large extent, whether or not the farmer would be able to borrow money to get the new venture underway.

In schooling professional staff typically resist monitoring—systematic collection of information—let alone evaluation of teachers, schools, programs or school systems. Teachers and principals complain about filling in reports. The province of Ontario recently opted out of a national program to monitor literacy and numeracy levels of 13-year-olds and 16-year-olds. The teachers' union in Western Australia opposed the implementation of state-mandated School Development Plans because they saw the monitoring component, particularly, as a ploy for accountability. It is interesting to note that as educators we regularly evaluate students and send home report cards but we get much more excited about the evaluation of the adults involved in schooling. The view of the writers is that we must begin to see monitoring and evaluation, not as punitive, but as an integral part of strategic planning and school development. Without accurate, relevant information we have no basis for making judgments about what is happening in schools nor about how to proceed further toward our preferred future—vision. A first step in establishing sound evaluation practices is to identify indicators of quality.

## Quality Indicators

In the business of schooling we have often had notions of a "good school," a "caring" climate or a "real" leader but they have not been made explicit. During the last decade results of research have enabled us to identify characteristics of effective schools. Public pressures have forced us to become more open and precise in what we mean by quality in schooling, hence, the need for quality indicators at many levels from the school to the international.

There are a number of different initiatives underway regarding quality or performance indicators. There is an International Educational Indicators project sponsored by OECD with attention being given to indicators of the environment, the resources, the processes and the effects of schooling. Within Canada, the Council of Ministers of Education has launched Educational Quality Indicators Projects with Alberta playing a leading role. In the United States, California has established state-wide indicators and in Missouri indicators of student performance have been established. In Western Australia, schools are expected to identify indicators of school development and use them as a basis for monitoring plans.

Indicators represent a widespread and concerted effort to clarify thoughts, to improve communication and to provide a basis for development in relation to schooling. When a school staff is challenged to identify indicators of a caring climate dialogue is improved and action becomes focused. If parents, students and teachers begin to list indicators of good discipline, understanding of various points of view is increased and the groundwork for action and development is prepared. The ultimate purpose of indicators is to contribute to school and system development although this may be overshadowed at times by questions of accountability.

Although emphasis upon indicators is relatively recent, some issues have surfaced and some trends are apparent. A useful review has been provided by McEwen and Chow (1991) in an article entitled "Issues in Implementing Indicator Systems," *Alberta Journal of Educational Research*. From this and other sources the following points about indicators are drawn:

1. It seems to be agreed that indicators should meet certain criteria ranging all the way from common sense to questions of validity or usefulness and reliability or consistency. Put simply, these considerations lead us to ask, "Is the indicator really an indicator and is it free of unexplained fluctuations?" We could ask if performance on standardized tests is a good indicator of learning in mathematics or if the gender of a principal is a good indicator of leadership. In the first case, many would say that standardized test results are too narrow and that they should not be used as the only indicator although they are reliable. In the second question, despite some recent studies, there would likely be some argument about the association between gender and leadership. Another criteria for indicators has to do with the practicality of collecting information. We may say that students' sexual behaviour is a good indicator of the effectiveness of a health program but it is not easy to collect information beyond counting pregnancies or recording the number of condoms sold. In addition to being useful, consistent and practical indicators should be agreed to by various partners in education.

2. Indicator systems, in many cases, have moved beyond attendance, enrolment and achievement on standardized tests. In fact, McEwen and Chow claim that indicator systems should give attention to context, inputs, processes and products if we are to have the information necessary to interpret student out-

comes. For example, if student achievement in final exams in senior sciences is improving we need to consider indicators of changes in the environment—such as fewer students with part-time jobs, in the inputs—such as new lab equipment, in processes—such as more emphasis on inquiry, that may be related to that outcome. In addition, we would probably want to consider indicators of teacher competence, student aptitude and achievement in other subject areas.

3. Interpretation of indicator system results is aided by considering clusters of indicators for each aspect of a vision or each goal. There could be five or six indicators of independent learning or a caring climate for instance. A further dimension is added when we recognize the need to hear the voices of all partners. Students could identify an indicator of a caring climate (no detention!), as could teachers, parents, administrators and support staff.

4. It is readily apparent that indicator systems can become complex and, in fact, overwhelming. In this regard it is vital to "think big and start small." A logical starting point is to collaboratively identify the indicators of success for three or four of the top priorities in the strategic plan. In this way the basis for monitoring, evaluation and effective change will be established. The results may be something along the lines of what is shown in Table 9.1. Do those indicators appear to be useful, consistent and practical? How close are they to what may be identified by partners in your context? Attention will now turn to monitoring and evaluation systems which are based upon quality indicators.

## Monitoring

In a basic sense we monitor to see what is going on. We go to the thermometer to check the temperature. We recently noticed on a Hutterite colony that there was a monitor on each cow to keep a record of food intake. Corporate executives prepare graphs of sales and pilots, fortunately, check instruments as they come in for a landing. In school organizations, for decades, we have monitored enrolment, attendance, finances and student performance on standardized tests. Monitoring is a part of our personal and professional life yet there are three major reasons why it deserves special attention in the 1990s.

Multiple Perspectives. In preliminary stages of work in many rural school systems the writers with colleagues have often made one-day visits to schools. During the day one of us would interview the principal and vice-principal, one would have discussions with teachers, one would concentrate on students and one would meet representatives of the parents and community in order to determine their views of the school. Can you imagine our dialogue as we journeyed back to the city and asked, "What is going on in Big Wheel School?" These experiences and societal trends have helped us to realize that schools are viewed from many perspectives and it is very difficult to determine what is going on in any school at a particular time. An elaboration of this point is provided in Table 9.2. We have all felt the increasing influence of societal and narrative perspectives in the last decade.

### Table 9.1 Quality Indicators of a "Caring Climate"

| Indicator Identified by: | Indicator - The extent to which: | Sources of Data |
|---|---|---|
| Students | · teachers know students by name | · monitor and record greetings in hallways for use of first name |
|  | · students enjoy school | · student narratives about what it's like to be at school |
| Parents | · teachers share good news | · tally of times teachers inform parents of student success |
|  | · students are "heard" when in trouble | · record conversations when disciplining and tally "talk time" for teacher and student |
| Teachers | · efforts are recognized | · observe and monitor staff meetings for forms of recognition |
|  | · living and learning are integrated | · teacher narratives of life at school during the month of November |
| Administrators | · there is less swearing, bullying, fighting | · tally of incidents |
|  | · there is more willingness to participate, assist | · participation and leadership in the co-curricular program |
| Community/ province | · more students stay in school | · line graph of percentage of school leavers |
|  | · increased participation of parents/community | · count of numbers who attend events at school |

## Table 9.2 Perspectives of Schooling

| Perspective | Members | Sources of Information | Issues/Priorities |
|---|---|---|---|
| Societal | governments | legislation, social trends | finance, achievement, accountability |
| Intentional | school boards | evaluation, budgets | planning, finance |
| Structural | administrators | legislation, policy manuals | efficiency, effectiveness, governance |
| Analytical | researchers | studies, reports | roles, change processes |
| Portrait | students, parents, teachers, principals | self-respect | relevance, success, jobs, careers |
| Narrative | public | opinion polls | cost, discipline, retention |
| Pressure groups | any or all of the above | multiple, focused | minority/equity issues |

The fact that schooling is viewed from many perspectives is sometimes referred to as multiple realities. This means that there is no single or "absolute truth" about what is going on in Big Wheel School—recall the teachers' views of the principal in Chapter 6. Everyone sees a different part of the picture and adds to our understanding of it. This realization makes monitoring much more difficult and accounts for the trend towards more naturalistic studies of schooling with an emphasis on insiders' views, site visits and what schooling means to various participants. There is attention to meaning as well as to measurement.

*Some teachers have double standards. One for them and one for us.*
*For example: we can't chew gum, they do; we can't swear, they do.*
- a student

**School Development**. An integral part of the school development policy in Western Australia is planning how progress towards the vision for school development can be monitored. One school development plan, for example, includes increased student self-discipline and a caring environment as part of their vision. Their document lists indicators of self-discipline and of a caring environment. An action plan which includes a monitoring plan is set forth. Monitoring in relation to school development is far more complicated than keeping track of enrolment and attendance;

yet it is vital if we are to have any assurance that schools are moving in agreed-upon directions.

**Issues and Accountability.** Increasingly schooling is being linked to social issues such as employment, performance in the international market, the environment, equity and health costs. Many school systems have responded with new programs in areas such as technical-vocational, health, science and gifted education but we typically push these innovations with extra support and attention in the beginning (commonly called "Front-end loading") then move on to something else. In system after system the monitoring and evaluation phases of change processes are neglected. Consequently, school leaders are not usually able to convince themselves nor anyone else that innovations have had the impact intended. It leaves schools vulnerable to criticism because they do not have relevant information to respond to critics. Having such information is one "strategy" of strategic planning. For example, leaders for schooling in rural areas know that there is concern about young people going to the city and having difficulty so we should have reliable information from recent graduates and school leavers. We know there are worries about the achievement of girls in senior math and science so we should have relevant data about the issue in our schools—action, enrolments, achievement and so on. Similar comments could be made about multigrades, second languages, basic skills, whole language and a host of other issues. The point we wish to stress is that part of our strategy for school development is to respond to relevant social issues by having monitoring systems in place to provide current, relevant information.

The issue of accountability should be faced directly. If a school development plan sets forth what is to be done and how progress is to be monitored, the successes and failures of the school are going to be "up front" for all to see. Within the teaching profession individuals are going to become openly and directly accountable to one another. The principal and each teacher, as well as support staff in many cases, will stipulate what they are going to do to build self-discipline in students and to contribute to a caring climate, for example. Monitoring systems will reveal that some things have been done and some have not. It is similar to a check made on students who have and who have not done their homework! One reason adults often resist monitoring is that they realize monitoring may be linked to evaluation and they do not know what will happen if they have not achieved what they set out to do. One way to provide support is to emphasize repeatedly that the primary underlying purpose of monitoring is to provide current, relevant information for development not to "nail" teachers, principals, or superintendents.

## Meaning—Purpose

Monitoring is systematically collecting information. "Systematic" is a key word because it elevates monitoring beyond "gut feelings" or subjective impressions that may be casually picked up from day-to-day. By being systematic we monitor indicators which have been set forth from various perspectives to provide comprehensive data and we do it at regular time intervals not only at times of crisis or peak performance.

The position of the writers is that the primary purpose of monitoring systems is to provide an information base for further development or related short-term action plans. Some say that this is monitoring performance. What creative writing did the grade fours do in first term? To what extent are grade nines using the resource centre? What proportion of native students take part in the co-curricular program?

Monitoring may, as in examples given, be driven by the school system's internal plans and priorities. Data collected depends upon elements of the vision for the school system and the priorities set forth in the development.

Some monitoring may be required because of external expectations. A government may want assurance that grants are being targeted to specific programs, that policy manuals are complete or that grade 10 students are receiving 1 000 hours of instruction per year. The focus of this monitoring is compliance. Local issues may require some monitoring of content and discussion in language learning, of discipline in a particular classroom or of attention to problem solving in mathematics—this too may be motivated by compliance to external pressures. There are times, too, when monitoring is done for diagnosis. Some teachers claim that standardized tests are best used for this purpose. Information from monitoring may be required to diagnose various problems in instruction, use of school facilities or teacher satisfaction, for example.

In summary, monitoring, whether for performance, compliance or diagnosis, is the systematic collection of information regarding the performance of an individual, a school or a school system. Its primary purpose is to provide data for development but, at times, monitoring may be for compliance or diagnosis.

# Evaluation

Making informal evaluations are an everyday occurrence for all of us. For example, we may decide that the coffee is too strong, our lawn looks dry or our bank manager is very helpful. During the past week we were asked to complete an evaluation form for hotel service, a conference and a local auto dealer. Students are evaluated daily in school and report cards are distributed three or four times a year, yet if a parent were to get 4 out of 10 for preparing dinner, or if our partner's employer were to call us in for an interview we would think that it was very unusual. Although we consider evaluation routine in many aspects of our life, when we are to be evaluated or when any part of schooling is to be evaluated we get excited. Evaluation is similar to fire—we need it but at times it may do more harm than good. The purpose of this section is to provide persuasive arguments that evaluation can be a servant rather than a master of schooling initiatives.

## Meaning

Indicator systems and monitoring should provide an information base for evaluation. We could decide that the percentage of students engaged in learning at a particular time is an indicator of a quality environment for learning. We could then gather that information systematically to know that the class average is, for instance, 75 percent. If we have decided that the number of school leavers is an indicator of a good high school, and monitoring from month to month reveals that 10 male and 3 female students have left out of a total of 150, we have some useful information but we have not evaluated. Evaluation differs from monitoring in that it is a process of making *judgments* about the value or worth of some aspect of schooling. Judgment requires some standard or record of past performance. If we know, for example, from the literature that in effective schools classes average 90 percent of their time engaged in learning we can judge that improvement is still necessary. If we note, however, that the same class averaged only 62 percent last month we can make a judgment about their progress. The point to be emphasized is that judgment is central to evaluation processes.

## Purposes

Whether we consider the informal, individual evaluation of a bank manager or the formal evaluation of a school system by an external team the purpose is to improve decision making. The individual is going to decide where to do banking and school authorities are going to decide on further school development, so they need an accurate portrayal of current, strengths and weaknesses. Evaluation feeds directly into the internal analysis of strategic planning.

In the current decade in a number of countries, evaluation of teachers, programs, schools and school systems is required for reasons of accountability and political gain. Periods of deficit budgets, economic restraint and rising public dissatisfaction with education increase pressures for sound, ongoing evaluation. Public attention to individual rights and equity highlights the importance of defensible student and teacher evaluation processes. Even these external demands and pressures are derived from the perceived need for improved decision making.

Within the general purpose of evaluation are two commonly used terms: *formative* evaluation is comprised of judgments we make day-by-day in order to guide behavior; *summative* evaluation is a summary of formative evaluations and it is usually somewhat final and recorded. A teacher makes many formative evaluations each day as students do mathematics but it is the summative evaluation that appears on the report card. Similarly, superintendents form evaluations of principals from time to time but summative evaluations are done only once a year or so and are reported in writing.

## Processes

As part of strategic planning evaluation is both preceded and followed by clarification of mission, environmental scanning, visioning, identification of indicators, implementation and monitoring in an ongoing process of school development. It is vital to see evaluation as a central part of a larger school development process. Evaluation is not an end in itself. It should be viewed as a continuous, natural part of learning and developing.

Various writers have identified steps in an evaluation process. While we realize that evaluation, like schooling, is much more complex and dynamic than "steps" indicate, we list the following for clarification of program, school or system evaluation processes:

1. Clarify the purpose of the evaluation. For whom is it intended? What decisions will it impact? Is it being driven by goals, issues, models or an examination of curriculum as lived? A repertoire of evaluation strategies is required to serve various purposes.

2. Identify the partners and give them a voice. Decide who is to do the evaluation and whether key questions will be asked in the beginning or after trends and issues have been identified.

3. Review indicators, determine sources of information and set time lines.

4. Plan for access to information. Prepare to collect data by interviews, journals, diaries, logs, questionnaires etc.

5. Collect and interpret information—make meaning.

6. Prepare a preliminary report and check with key participants.

7. Present a final report, discuss and communicate.

8. Plan and conduct follow-up.

After a particularly successful system evaluation, Newton and McKinnon (1990) emphasized the importance of a close working relationship between Ministry and system officials, involvement of partners, the key role of the chair of an evaluation team, a model to help people see how different aspects are related, credibility of evaluators, the need for leadership, sustained support and the follow-up phase which they found requires as much time and as many resources as the evaluation itself. They found that the strengths listed were necessary in order to conduct a quality evaluation and also to overcome difficulties during the process. They were challenged to clarify the role of the school board, to gain trustees' consent to be observed at a meeting, to overcome administrators' reluctance to have a leadership inventory used and to have all team members agree to the content of the final report. It should be noted that in Alberta the government requires school systems to adopt and implement policy for student, teacher, program, school and system evaluation, and regional office personnel assist school jurisdictions in the process. In the case reported here, McKinnon and Newton, superintendent and Ministry official respectively, were determined to move beyond compliance and link the evaluation to school development. One year after the evaluation was completed, 71 percent of the report had been acted on, 13 percent was in process and 16 percent had not yet received attention.

School and system evaluations are expensive in terms of time required, costs and tensions produced so it is particularly important to identify indicators of quality evaluations. Some indicators such as involvement of stakeholders, credibility of evaluators and extent of follow-up (integration into a strategic planning process) have been mentioned. In addition, the evaluation needs to be focused on strategic issues, useful and practical. Usefulness often hinges on having outcomes of the evaluation data-based and specific. Practicality includes not only the feasibility of collecting the information but also the possibility of seriously following-up the out-comes.

> *I feel that some 'Evaluation' time is wasted and fewer evaluations*
> *would not reduce the effectiveness of our schools. We do not need*
> *outside people investigating our schools constantly.*
> - a teacher

Historically evaluation in educational organizations has been difficult and typically neglected except for the evaluation of students. In the 1980s calls for reform in education have often been met with more emphasis on standards and external evaluation as though the added constraints and pressure will magically improve learning and schooling. A frustrated educator from the United Kingdom in responding to such trends said in the fall of 1990, "Our students are not doing well and by God we're going to know it!" The challenge for leaders in schooling is to be "a jump ahead" of these environmental pressures so that evaluation, internal and external, can be integrated usefully into the strategic planning process. With that conviction in mind we summarize this section with a review of trends and considerations.

## Trends and Considerations

1. Organizations are viewed as moving ahead (perhaps even against a current), in circles or drifting backwards. Some say schools are either moving or stuck. The need is to be action-oriented within the strategic planning process. Act, evaluate and improve.

2. Effective personnel, programs, schools and systems require evaluation every bit as much as do the less effective. Evaluation provides fuel for continuous growth.

3. There is a much improved knowledge base and support structure for evaluation than there was a decade ago. The literature is plentiful regarding effective schools, teachers, leaders and change processes. Ministry and university personnel are typically available to assist. (Universities also are being challenged to be effective and of service to the society from which they draw support.)

4. Comparisons are necessary in some areas and evaluation of performance against provincial, national and even interna-

tional standards will continue to be required by all levels of governments. Those pressures will not diminish in the 1990s as developed countries place increased emphasis on human capital. Leaders for schooling in sparsely populated areas need to incorporate results from these externally-driven evaluations into their strategic plans and balance them with internal evaluations.

5. There are strong moves in developed countries, and particularly among advocates of small schools, to have more evaluations that emphasize the local context, insiders' views and what schooling means from the perspective of various partners. Words are given the same attention as numbers and meaning is given the same weight as measurement. Such approaches to evaluation and research are called "naturalistic" because they focus on "ordinary people" under natural conditions. We strongly endorse such approaches.

6. Human rights and legal considerations require thorough evaluation procedures. Care must be given to due process and respect for all concerned. In other words, evaluation must be directly linked to improvement, it must be data based and time and support for subsequent development must be provided before another evaluation takes place.

7. It is important to lead by example and to have the performance of superintendents and school boards evaluated as part of the strategic planning process.

Many school systems are conducting exemplary evaluations. Illustrations follow.

## Turning to Illustrations

Four examples of developments in relation to monitoring and evaluation are reported. Two are at the state level, one is on a naturalistic approach to program evaluation and the fourth is a brief summary of a comprehensive system review.

## Figure 9.1 Elementary School Library Program Evaluation

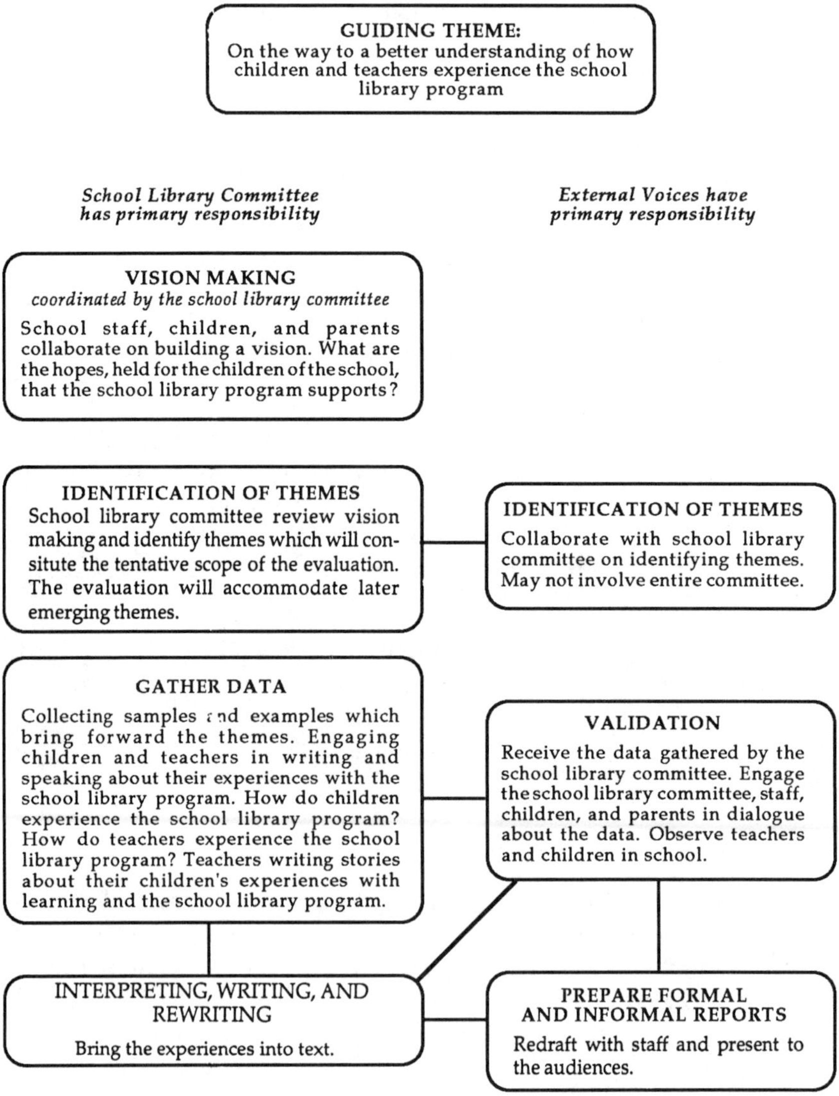

**GUIDING THEME:**
On the way to a better understanding of how children and teachers experience the school library program

*School Library Committee has primary responsibility*

*External Voices have primary responsibility*

**VISION MAKING**
*coordinated by the school library committee*

School staff, children, and parents collaborate on building a vision. What are the hopes, held for the children of the school, that the school library program supports?

**IDENTIFICATION OF THEMES**
School library committee review vision making and identify themes which will consitute the tentative scope of the evaluation. The evaluation will accommodate later emerging themes.

**IDENTIFICATION OF THEMES**
Collaborate with school library committee on identifying themes. May not involve entire committee.

**GATHER DATA**
Collecting samples and examples which bring forward the themes. Engaging children and teachers in writing and speaking about their experiences with the school library program. How do children experience the school library program? How do teachers experience the school library program? Teachers writing stories about their children's experiences with learning and the school library program.

**VALIDATION**
Receive the data gathered by the school library committee. Engage the school library committee, staff, children, and parents in dialogue about the data. Observe teachers and children in school.

**INTERPRETING, WRITING, AND REWRITING**
Bring the experiences into text.

**PREPARE FORMAL AND INFORMAL REPORTS**
Redraft with staff and present to the audiences.

Alberta Education: Calgary Regional Office

In 1987 the Ministry of Education in Western Australia developed a position paper entitled "Better Schools in Western Australia: A Programme for Improvement." Following that, Policy and Guidelines for School Development Plans stipulated that the plans must include the purpose of the school, indicators of the school's performance, details of how the school will monitor its performance, local and Ministry priorities, how priorities will be addressed and how resources will be allocated. School Development Plans must include participation of parents to provide accountability to the community and they must be presented to the District Superintendent to demonstrate accountability to government. The District Office provides leadership and support for this initiative. Interviews and review of plans from four rural schools indicate that plans are taking shape as intended. It is too early to know to what extent they are implemented and principals are struggling to integrate the "top down" and "bottom up" components.

The State of Missouri School Improvement Program includes a Standards and Indicators Manual. There are 56 suggested indicators for curriculum and instruction and 94 for governance and administration, for example. Indicators of the expected development of school district philosophy and goals include: involvement of staff, parents and community; being based upon needs of youth and adults; reflecting a democratic spirit; provision for review as conditions change; availability to the public; knowledge and understanding of staff; awareness of students and community. The State standards for improvement are applied to each school site for evaluation. The related plans for improvement may include local indicators. Input and process indicators are to be included as well as output indicators. State authorities then classify each school as "approved," "probation" or "unapproved."

A 1989 review of a rural school system in Alberta was initiated by the Superintendent and conducted by the Regional Office of the Ministry. The Steering Committee included two Ministry personnel, the Superintendent, the Chair and Vice-Chair of the Board, an Alberta Teachers' Association representative, two principals, the plant operations Manager and the Secretary-Treasurer. The general purpose of the evaluation was to determine where the school system stood on the continuum of goal attainment and to provide baseline data for subsequent studies. Particular attention was given to provision of learning opportunities appropriate for each student, facilities, governance, planning for renewal and partnerships. The 18-member evaluation team included five Ministry officials, an executive of the Royal Bank, a human resource manager from Shell Canada, a board chair from another school system, a secretary-treasurer from another system, five administrators from neighbouring jurisdictions, a principal from the system, a university faculty member, a representative of the Alberta School Trustees Association and a private consultant. Data were gathered from the 15 schools, teachers, students, parents and community by interviews, questionnaires, observations and document analysis. Commendations in the final report were related to the openness of the Board to a thorough review, the mission statement, focus on students' needs, caring climate in schools, student achievement, teacher competence, supportive principals, a sense of trusteeship, financial management and policies for release of information. Areas for growth were identified to be: communication among central office, schools and trustees; human resource development; monitoring and review of policies; the development of a comprehensive strategic planning process.

In our view the examples presented are representative of important developments in the provinces of western Canada, in Australia and in the United States. Many school systems in sparsely populated areas are well into the development and use of indicators, monitoring systems and ongoing evaluation processes as components of strategic planning.

*There is room for improvement in some areas, but I think the
school has been doing the best possible job it can do with the limited amount of teachers, money, room and other facilities it has.
It could stand more involvement from the parents' side . . .*

- a parent

## References

Alberta Education (1988). *County system review*. Calgary Regional Office.

— (1989). *School division system review*. Calgary Regional Office.

— (1990). *Educational quality indicators: Inventory of assessment instruments*. Corporate and Fiscal Planning, Edmonton.

— (1990). *Educational quality indicators: Methodological considerations*. Corporate and Fiscal Planning, Edmonton.

— (1990). *Elementary School library program evaluation*. Calgary Regional Office.

Carkhuff, R. (1988). *The age of the new capitalism*. Amherst MA: Human Resources Development Press, Inc.

McEwen, N. & Chow, H. (1991). *Issues in implementing indicator systems. Alberta Journal of Educational Research*, 37(1), 65-86.

Missouri State Board of Education. (1990). *Missourians prepared: Success for every student*. Jefferson City.

Newton, P. & McKinnon, G. (1990). *School system evaluation: Two perspectives.* A paper presented to the Canadian Society for the Study of Education, Victoria, June.

Newton, E. & Hopkirk, G. (1986). *Reconstructing educational organizations: Reason and foolishness required*. The Canadian School Executive, 6(2), 3-12.

Richards, C.E. (1988). *Educational monitoring systems: Implications for design*. Phi Delta Kappan, 69(7), 495-499.

Van Mannen, M. (1990). *Researching lived experience: Human science for an action sensitive pedagogy*. London, Ontario: The Althouse Press.

Western Australia Ministry of Education (1987). *Better schools in Western Australia: A programme for improvement*. Perth.

— (1989). *School development plans: Policy and guidelines*. Perth.

— (1990). *School decision making - Policy and guidelines*. Perth.

— (1991 Draft). *School accountability: Policy and guidelines*. Perth.

Worthen, B. & Sanders, D. (1987). *Educational evaluation: Alternative approaches and practical guidelines*. New York: Longman.

# SECTION FOUR

# Putting It All Together

We found in writing this book that we had to sort out and make explicit some of our beliefs as a starting point. By the same token we think it is vital for a leader to pause from time to time and write down beliefs that are key to schooling. The next step is to ask how things related to those beliefs could be better in a school system and what action should be taken. In the following pages we present our model of strategic planning within which we have integrated the ideas in this book. We have put together a type of worksheet for each phase of strategic planning on which we invite you to note your beliefs, ideas for relating to partners and plans for the school system.

# 10

# A Learning Organization

*I was not clear at the start of the Preferred Futures meeting as
to what would happen. But people got pretty excited. I
got the impression, though, that not much would happen.*

- a parent

We have noted that in many ways traditional school organizations are more complicated than business and industrial enterprises: goals are ambiguous, there is a low level of interdependence among staff, they are vulnerable to attack, evaluation is difficult and they have not had to compete for survival. In addition, school organizations were created in a much more stable, predictable environment than we have today. The dominant beliefs then had to do with absolute truths, authority, discipline and strictly academic pursuits. As part of the industrial age, control and efficiency were emphasized resulting in a "bigger is better" value system. We are now living in a dynamic, global community where traditional organizational structures are no longer appropriate. We see businesses emphasizing flexibility, participation, strategic planning, and webs of communication rather than levels of authority. Our contention is that we must redesign schools for sparsely populated areas and that strategic planning is a promising approach for revitalizing learning for all groups in small school-communities.

*We live in a rural area not by choice but by heritage. Do not
attempt to break down our sense of worth and belonging by
centralizing. It fragments our society and family. Do respect our needs
for a standard one would receive automatically in a larger centre.*

- a parent

The model of strategic planning which we have in mind is shown in Figure 10.1 and a summary of each phase is presented in the pages which follow. We expect that each leader who examines the model would modify it by adding descriptors, circles or lines. Similarly, we have left space for your notes and comments on the summary pages. For example, we have highlighted a line that connects monitoring—evaluation with internal analysis because all too often people see evaluation as an end in itself. It is not the details of the model that are important but rather the intent of strategic planning which in our view includes the following:

- to make organizations more responsive to a changing environment

- to link global—national—local factors

- to integrate activities toward a preferred future and thereby give them meaning

- to monitor and evaluate growth and so provide information capital for continual renewal

- to stress openness, participation and leadership

## Figure 10.1 Strategic Planning for School System Development

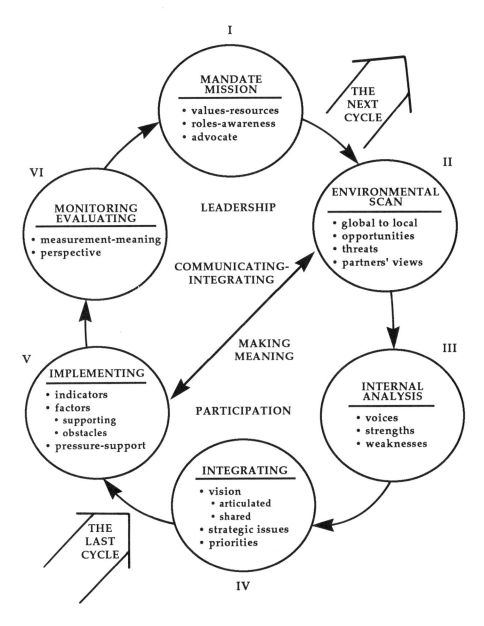

Earle Newton and Patti Newton, 1991

# Mission—Mandate for Strategic Planning

**Thinking**

Strategic planning (SP) is an information system that enables one to take changing conditions into consideration when making decisions and to link today's action to visions of tomorrow. The purpose is to have schools and school systems systematically moving towards a preferred future.

To what extent are you, the board and central office administrators, aware of the meaning and potential of SP? To what extent is it implemented?

Is there a system mandate for development (change) which entails some risk or does the board prefer that they "keep the lid on" and play it safe? Is the system really focused on students?

Are there resources (human and financial) to support it and an advocate to "see it through" and maintain momentum?

What is my personal position regarding SP? People will feel they can trust me if they know my position on vital matters.

**Relating**

Are there people I need to talk to either to extend my own thoughts or to lay the groundwork for action at the system level?

Am I willing to really dialogue—to bring my basic beliefs and assumptions to the surface for examination?

Can we in a group set forth guiding principles for action?

**Planning**

This is the level of leaders building a learning organization. Expectations and processes for continual learning are built in so that the organization continues to learn even if key people leave.

Is each phase of the SP process incorporated into the policies, roles, budget and operation of the school system? If so, is it strong and central? If not, an implementation plan is needed.

**Notes**

# Environmental Scan

**Thinking**

School systems are closely linked to and dramatically affected by developments and issues from the global to the local scene. Wheat prices and environmental issues are examples.

How is your school system affected by the local economy, population shifts, ethnic diversity, technology and other community issues?

Does your system have a process to systematically and comprehensively monitor trends and developments that affect it?

In your view, what opportunities and threats are presented in the external environment? Are we realizing the potential advantages of small schools?

**Relating**

Do I need to meet with or get information from community development agencies, health authorities, business leaders or cultural groups? Are community leaders seeing the school as an integral part of community development or do I need to open up some informal dialogue?

**Planning**

Do system policies and role descriptions provide for systematic monitoring of the environment, related dialogue and integration into the SP process? If so, is it working? If not, let's plan to begin. School-community integration is a major potential advantage in sparsely populated areas.

**Notes**

## Internal Analysis—Voices

**Thinking**

Emphasis has been placed upon the voices of students, parents, community, teachers and administrators both informally and formally so that the differing views about what is currently going on in the school system may be heard. People from each perspective also respond willingly to questions about what needs to be changed so that the journey towards a preferred future may begin or continue.

As a leader what picture do you see when you hear all the voices and put the messages together with your own observations? What do you see as system strengths and areas for growth?

**Relating**

It may be that you need to have more dialogue and conversation with particular stakeholder groups to better understand how they see things. An informal meeting with student, teacher, parent or community leaders may be helpful.

Is there a need for a meeting to put together a composite picture?

**Planning**

Does the system have procedures in place to systematically and regularly hear the voices of all stakeholders? Equally important are the leadership and resources for follow-up—integration into the SP process.

**Notes**

## Visioning

**Thinking**

The word "visioning" highlights the aspect of leadership which entails "seeing how things could be better". The other major aspect of leadership—human relations, is emphasized in the relating and planning parts of strategic planning. *Personal vision is the first step toward building a shared, articulated vision for a system.*

What aspects do I care most about when I imagine how things could be better in our school system?

As I link the present to the future—see the gap between "what is" and "what could be"—do I get motivated? What personal investment am I going to make? Do I want to be a leader?

**Relating**

Personal positions and dialogue will lead to refocusing and refinement of personal visions. As environmental scanning is reviewed in relation to internal analysis, and as the present is compared to the future, strategic issues will emerge—the most important considerations in your school system in preparing young people for the next century.

**Planning**

At this point the school system builds upon recommendations from education partners to decide on priorities and a strategic planning process that will be communicated widely as a means for annual renewal. In this way the vision of the system will be articulated and shared. The vision will give meaning to the daily activities of everyone in the school system as they will see how they are contributing to development.

**Notes**

## Implementing

**Thinking**

*3 years?*

Implementation is the phase in the change process when words are put into action. Things do not just happen. Change includes overcoming barriers and coping with anxiety. The challenge for leaders is to do strategic planning so the system is able to build upon strengths and reduce barriers.

Consider a curriculum or organizational change that is underway in your school system and list the factors which are affecting it either positively or negatively.

Are these same factors likely to be the ones that will affect the school system as it attempts to develop towards the vision?

*In your opinion* what are the most important factors?

**Relating**

To build upon potential positive factors for implementation such as having strong leadership from teachers you will need to meet the teacher leaders early in the formulation of a strategic plan. Similarly, if you anticipate objections from parents, you will need to make special efforts to provide opportunities in the sharing of information and having dialogue. Many groups would need to be involved in identifying indicators.

**Planning**

The strategic plans for implementation are going to have to go to the board for consideration, approval and support. There are almost certain to be adjustments in role description and in the budget, for instance.

Is the support of central office visible and strong?

**Notes**

# Monitoring—Evaluation

**Thinking**

This area is a major challenge for school organizations as we tend to "front-end load" and neglect these more difficult aspects of strategic planning. We have stressed the importance of identifying indicators of quality as a first step in monitoring and evaluation.

Does your system have current information regarding strategic issues and system priorities?

How can evaluation become a more integral part of SP?

Is there a balance between external and internal evaluation and between measurement and meaning?

What is my position regarding information capital and the purposes of evaluation? Do stakeholders know where I stand?

**Relating**

Indicators are important in doing environmental scans, in internal analysis and in planning for implementation so many have likely been identified in dialogue in earlier stages of the SP process. It is important to keep indicators "up front" in relating to various stakeholders. Monitoring and evaluation create pressure which must be balanced with support for stakeholder groups. Leaders provide support by meeting such groups to share views regarding how monitoring and evaluation link to development.

**Planning**

Does the school jurisdiction have a monitoring system in place which is directly related to evaluation and SP?

Are there appropriate human and material resources allocated to these functions?

Are the superintendent and board setting an example by establishing indicators, monitoring and evaluating their own performance?

**Notes**

*We 'flip-flop' so much as a board.*

- a trustee

## Dealing with a Dilemma

We have all at times been "tough" in leadership roles and, at other times, "soft." We can sense from our experience and from observing leaders in action that there are times for both. Peters and Waterman almost a decade ago used the expression "simultaneous loose-tight" and Huberman (1983) has called effective leadership a combination of "muscle, tenderness and tutoring." We have seen some board members and superintendents very skillfully combine being "loose" and being "tight" whereas others get into no end of difficulty by "backing down" at the wrong time in relation to a vital issue or by "remaining adamant" when flexibility is called for. The change process, for example, inevitably includes some anxiety and opposition, causing weak leaders to downsize the innovation or quit pushing so that very little is accomplished. Strong leaders, on the other hand, can "take the flack" and balance the pressures people feel with various forms of organizational support. Recall the case of Mr. Strong in Chapter 8 on change processes.

The loose-tight dilemma can be more specifically linked to the strategic planning process. In relation to the mission-mandate, leaders are *loose* during dialogue when various possibilities are being considered but once the various aspects of mission-mandate are agreed to they are put in writing and communicated—they are *tight* until the next review. Only in this way can all stakeholders know what is expected of them—it is a type of security. The environmental scanning and internal analysis require an openness to all points of view in the early stages but eventually dialogue must *narrow down* to a manageable list of opportunities, threats, strengths and weaknesses. These *do not become set*, however, because dramatic events could change the situation any day. The integration requires open dialogue as alternative futures are formulated and thought about. After a reasonable time strategic issues are identified, priorities are established and a vision is articulated and shared. Like the mission-mandate, the vision becomes *set* as an agreed upon direction until the next review period. When it comes to implementing, monitoring and evaluating leaders are *tight* in terms of their expectations but *loose* in relation to details of implementation as methods can best be determined by the professional staff. Effective school systems can therefore be described as simultaneously loose-tight. Strong leaders are firm regarding agreed to mandates, priorities, vision, changes, monitoring and evaluation—that is the muscle. They are tender and offer various forms of support (tutoring) for the processes of strategic planning and for the professional staff who have to implement, monitor and evaluate. There is more to leadership than leaving people alone or concentrating on keeping them happy. There has to be clarity of mandate and then pressure in terms of vision and high expectations for its realization combined with various forms of support. Put another way, teacher empowerment is preceded by vision, priorities and expected changes and it is followed by monitoring and evaluation—a tight-loose-tight sequence.

*Capitalizing on Context*

A central purpose of this book is to better connect the school and the community in sparsely populated areas through effective strategic planning processes. We hope to have persuaded readers that small schools are not inevitably second rate compared to larger, urban schools. Illustrations of effective schooling in response to local conditions have been presented throughout this book. Some of examples are summarized in Table 10.2 to remind us of many effective small schools. We can all recall visiting and being a part of small school systems which featured voices of stakeholders, a shared vision and a sense of vitality through continual renewal and development. Leaders in these systems engaged in strategic planning. They were "tight" in relation to high expectations, priorities and the requirement that development must take place. They were "loose" in terms of listening, dialogue and supporting professional staff. They were moving towards a learning organization.

# Back to the Learning Organization

What we have been stressing in this book has been said succinctly by Senge (1990):

> *At the heart of a learning organization is a shift of mind—from seeing ourselves as separate from the world to connected to the world, from seeing problems caused by someone or something 'out there' to seeing how our own actions create the problems we experience. A learning organization is where people are continually discovering how they create their own reality. And how they can change it. (p. 12-13)*

### Table 10.2 Capitalizing on the Context
### of Small School Communities

| Context | Capitalizing |
|---|---|
| **Typical Advantages** | |
| · small population | · school-community integration |
| · people know each other well | · locally relevant curriculum |
| | · hands on learning in the real world |
| · low pupil-teacher ratios | · individual attention |
| · teacher generalists | · more student participation in discussion, leadership etc. |
| · multigrades | · peer coaching, co-operative learning |
| | · program continuity |
| · small operation | · clearer, stronger voices of stakeholders |
| · administrators well known | · enhanced parent-community involvement |
| | · change is faster—less "red tape" |
| **Typical Disadvantages** | |
| · isolation | · vision for a sense of "pulling together" |
| · local politics and values | · monitoring and evaluation for realization of progress |
| | · need strong information systems for environmental scanning |
| | · distance education for total community |
| · teacher recruitment, retention | · incentives re: housing, leadership opportunities etc. |
| · professional development | · professional development, networks |
| | · far-sighted personnel policies, exchanges, etc. |
| · vulnerability to personnel changes | · a learning organization involving all stakeholders |

## In Conclusion

We hope that in this book we have articulated and shared our personal vision for better schools in sparsely populated areas—schools that have become learning organizations through strategic planning processes. Such schools capitalize on context, so that learning is an ongoing process for everyone in the school-community and leading is built into the organization to serve learners of all ages for years to come.

# References

Huberman, M. (1983). School Development Strategies that Work. *Educational Leadership*, 4(3), 21-25.

Peters, T. & Waterman, R. (1982). *In search of excellence.* New York: Harper & Row, Inc.

Senge, P. (1990). *The fifth discipline: The act and practice of the learning organization.* Toronto: Doubleday Currency.

Printed in Canada